To the residents of Southdown

Bob Holman is one of the most important social reformers of his generation. He insists on staying close to the community which he has striven to help while still being familiar with the latest research. His views always reflect those of the poor and disadvantaged people whom he has taken as his point of reference. He has always retained integrity, a sense of humour and, perhaps most important of all, optimism.

Malcolm Dean
Former SDP parliamentary candidate for Bath
Editor Guardian Society

During the first eight years I spent as Member of Parliament in Bath I got to know Bob Holman and the community project he ran with the support of the Children's Society in one of the city's biggest council estates at Southdown. Bob's work in Southdown was one of the best examples of a neighbourhood project. Working on the spot with youngsters from disadvantaged backgrounds trying to help them negotiate a moderately successful passage through the hazardous years of growing up.

Unlike many social scientists Bob has now come back to Southdown to see what happened to the young people he worked with. The results are fascinating and underline the importance of deep-rooted community work.

The Rt Hon Christopher Patten C H
Former Conservative MP for Bath

The problems of a particular community are often best solved by those who live in a community. But such people need to be empowered to develop the solutions. Bob Holman and his Southdown Project team – living and working in the Southdown neighbourhood in Bath – provided that empowerment. This fascinating book shows how, years later, the success of the project can be judged by the lives of those its work touched. If, like me, you are wary about 'top-down' solutions, this book shows that the 'bottom-up' approach can and does work.

Don Foster MP
Liberal Democrat, Bath

The Southdown Project, gave hope and possibility to young people who thought they had neither. If the government really wants to revitalise communities, divert youngsters from crime, render neighbourhoods safe, then Bob Holman should be its guru.

Baroness Helena Kennedy QC
Labour Peer

Kids at the Door

Revisited

A follow-up into adulthood of young people
who were associated with a community project
on their council estate.

BOB HOLMAN

Russell House Publishing

First published in 2000 by:
Russell House Publishing Ltd.
4 St. George's House
The Business Park
Uplyme Road
Lyme Regis
Dorset DT7 3LS

Tel: 01297 443948
Fax: 01297 442722
e-mail: help@russelhouse.co.uk

British Library cataloguing-in-publication data:
A catalogue record for this book is available from the British Library.

ISBN: 1-898924-58-9

Typeset by The Hallamshire Press Limited, Sheffield

Printed by Cromwell Press, Trowbridge

Russell House Publishing Limited

is a group of social work, probation, education and youth and community work practitioners working in close collaboration with a professional publishing team. Our aim is to work closely with the field to produce innovative and valuable materials to help managers, trainers, practitioners and students. We are keen to receive feedback on publications and new ideas for future projects.

Contents

Foreword

Few workers maintain contact with the young people who attend their projects. By interviewing 51 of them, now in their mid-thirties, Bob Holman has produced a unique assessment of the impact of a community project on their lives.

The scene is set in the first chapters with carefully monitored details that act as a salutary reminder of the importance of carefully reported research. The book then bursts into life as Bob weaves his vivid personal anecdotes into the young people's own stories of their lives. He goes on to draw out the essence of the project and to present ideas that I have already seen begin to make a difference in the outlook of people, young and old, in the town where I live.

I am told that what he describes does not fit easily with contemporary government approaches that have the following limitations:

- they impose policies from above
- they do not give priority to a mixed or neighbourhood-wide approach
- they favour swift intervention over slow diversion; and seem unaware of the value of long-term projects
- they advocate a professional, highly regulated system that may engender bureaucracy and stifle creativity.

The author, who was formerly Professor at Bath University and is now Visiting Professor at University of Glasgow in Social Policy while maintaining a major commitment to neighbourhood work there on the Easterhouse council estate, wants the government to encourage alternatives...

> *Unfortunately, the basic ingredients of the Southdown Project are not fashionable today. But if a National Neighbourhood Fund or a reformed National Lottery were to support such projects, a new generation would benefit in like manner to their predecessors on the Southdown estate.*

In the meantime, those of us who have a sense of neighbourhood – and play an active role – have to choose whether to 'jack it in' or 'have a go' on our own initiative with few if any resources. At least we now have Bob's experience to guide us, and the considerable encouragement that comes from reading this work.

Geoffrey Mann
Managing Director, Russell House Publishing
Project Leader, Working with Young People, Lyme Regis Development Trust
Management Committee Member, Lyme Regis Club for Young People

Chapter One

Kids at the Door

Introduction

In 1976, I left a university post to initiate a community project on the Southdown council estate, Bath. As an academic who had previously been a local authority child care officer, I had concluded that social workers too often lived outside of the very areas where they worked. I noted that estates and inner city areas often lacked facilities for young people. Living close to Southdown, I was able to talk with some people in the locality about my ideas. Two charitable trusts agreed to provide funds for a project while the Church of England Children's Society (later called just the Children's Society) agreed to oversee it. In 1976, my family moved into a house – once the doctor's surgery – in Southdown and the Southdown Project was under way. Its stated objectives were to provide youth amenities, to prevent children being taken into public care, and to help potential and actual delinquents. In time these objectives were widened to serve the whole neighbourhood. The basis of the approach was simply that I would be there and would work closely with residents.

The Early Years

Initially the staff consisted of myself and a part-time secretary. The latter was Audrey Browne who became much more than a secretary and for years was to be a helper and friend. Before I had moved in, I had got to know Dave Wiles. He was an unemployed young man, born and bred in Southdown, a former delinquent who had experienced a Christian conversion. Dave was eager to be involved and became the first chair of the senior youth club. Later, funds were raised to take him on as an assistant worker. The youth club had started after I had knocked on almost every door on the estate and hung about chatting with youngsters. Parents most wanted something to stop the kids making trouble in the streets. The youngsters were bored and wanted a club. Initially it met in our home and then found a base in Hallett's Studios, a run-down, freezing cold, prefab. When the club had to leave there it moved to the Ascension church hall, just outside of Southdown, and then into St Barnabas's church hall on the estate.

In 1981, *Kids at the Door* was published as a record of the first three years of the Southdown Project. It showed that the work had expanded rapidly with youth clubs for various ages, sports teams, day trips, holidays. Jane Sellars joined the team and immediately made an impact as she developed activities with girls and young mothers. Later, Jim Davis, another young man who had spent all his life on the estate, was also added to the staff. Although the clubs were held in church halls, the house remained the hub of the project and the book revealed that in the three years, there were 1,596 knocks on the door from youngsters and adults. The knocks were answered by the staff (or leaders as they were usually called) and by my wife, Annette, and our children Ruth and David. The calls were usually for straightforward information about what the clubs were doing but they played a part in building up the individual relationships which were to be so central to the work

By the end of the initial three years, the house was bursting at its seams. The mothers and toddlers groups met there, at lunch time soup was served to teenagers who were then taken back to school in the minibus, youngsters gathered in the evenings and much of the clubs' equipment, the sports gear and the camping tents were stored there. Residents began to call for a building. I was initially dubious. What building? Apart from the church and schools there were no buildings suitable for a project. What about the costs? Would a move from the house change the homely ethos? But the demand grew. The Children's Society was agreeable and was prepared to meet half the costs. A local fund-raising committee was established. After long negotiations, Bath City Council made available a plot of land (next to the public toilets) at the foot of Roundhill, a grassy, sloping, open space. The money was raised. In 1983, the purpose built centre was opened. Most of the clubs transferred there although much still happened at the house. Cathy Bright joined the team on a temporary basis and gave attention to the elderly members of the community. Meanwhile Dave Wiles – after studying to catch up on his 'O' and 'A' levels – was seconded to Bristol University to take the Diploma in Social Work. While he was away, Tim Tappenden took his place.

Change of Leadership

On his return from university, Dave took over from me as the main leader. I stayed on still working in the clubs but was also able to give more time to relationships with individuals. After ten years, the project was fully established with local leadership. I felt nicely redundant. Our own children had left home for college.

Annette and I moved to her native Glasgow where we settled on the Easterhouse estate and soon became involved in another project. The Southdown Project became known as the Roundhill Project but I will continue to use the former name. It prospered under Dave's leadership. He was a much more effective and efficient manager than I had been. I had coped with running clubs, relating with residents and raising money but I had never excelled as a team leader, administrator and trainer. Dave showed such a range of abilities that in 1989 the Children's Society promoted him as assistant regional director with a wider brief in the west of England. In like manner, Jane Sellars and Jim Davis also later transferred to different work with the Children's Society. However as Dave and Jim still lived in the area, they were able to maintain many of their contacts with the project. A Community Association had been established and it elected a Management Committee to oversee the project. Therese Mitchell (a local parent) and Chris Park (a former youth club member) became the paid leaders with other residents in sessional posts. By this time, the Children's Society was withdrawing their involvement and the committee successfully obtained a grant from the local authority. After several years, Therese and Chris left for other posts. They were succeeded by Lynn Bragg who brought in new ideas and initiated a well equipped play area outside of the building. But the funding situation deteriorated as the local authority cut its contribution. The project survived with volunteers until, in 1997, the Bath YMCA took over and revived it. What follows in this book will concentrate on the years 1976–1986, the years in which I was present and kept records of every call, every interview, and every activity. This is not meant to undervalue what happened subsequently and what will happen in the future.

The Study

In this book I will write about 'children', usually meaning those aged 12 and under, 'young people', meaning teenagers aged 13–19, and 'youngsters' as a generic term for them all. However, at times, the terms will be used interchangeably and sometimes I will slip into calling them 'kids'. After moving to Glasgow, Annette and I kept in contact with some of our Southdown friends. A small number came to visit us, others phoned or wrote or sent a Christmas card. Being interested in them, I wanted to know how they were turning out. It occurred to me that their experiences with the Southdown Project might be of interest to others. It was time to revisit those kids at the door. The basic question I am asking is 'What effect did the Southdown Project have on the youngsters who came to it?' In *Kids at the Door*, I gave some case examples which indicated that a number of youngsters had been helped to counter their anti-social behaviour – and a few who had not.

But this was just over three years. What happened to the youngsters as they got into their older teens and into adulthood? Moreover, I wanted to know, once they became adults, how they regarded the Southdown Project, what they saw as its value, if any, and what they perceived as making for its successes or failures. The trustees and the director, Eric Adams, of the Barrow Cadbury Trust considered that the study proposal was a valuable one in that it might throw light on what factors help youngsters in deprived areas and an unusual one in that it followed users up into adulthood. The trust therefore made me a grant to undertake an investigation with the objectives stated as,

- to assess what former members thought about the Southdown Project and its staff, what they considered they gained, if anything, from it, and what they regarded as its useful characteristics.
- to ascertain what had happened to them as adults.
- to assess the effects, if any, the project had on them and their peers both as youngsters and as adults.

During the years 1976–86, the Southdown Project had contact with hundreds of children and young people. They attended the clubs, played in the sports teams, came on the trips and the holidays. Which ones should I attempt to interview in order to carry out the study? I kept a detailed diary over the years and it emerged that many were club participants and that was all. Others drew closer, came to the activities for years, became regular callers at the house and knew the leaders well. In nearly all instances, their parents were also familiar with the project leaders. Those in close contact, I numbered at 88 and I decided they should be the core of the study. By 1998, they were all in their late twenties to mid thirties. How could they be reached? A few had kept in touch with me over the years. Dave Wiles, Jane Sellars and Jim Davis still knew a larger number. The *Bath Chronicle* ran a feature and photo on the proposed follow-up and several former youngsters then phoned me. As I met some so they put me in touch with others. One initial finding that surprised and saddened me was that seven of the 88 were dead (and one died subsequently). In short, nine per cent of this very young age group had died. The reasons were cancer, a heart attack, cystic fibrosis and a thrombosis, a motor bike accident, a drug overdose, a fire, and murder. Of the remaining 81 (I interviewed one who later died), 16 could not be traced, 14 had letters sent to them and did not respond and 51 were interviewed. In short, around two thirds of those alive, were contacted and interviewed. I call them 'the study sample' or 'the study group'. In conjunction with the former leaders, I compiled an interview schedule which covered the respondents' early family lives, their experiences at school and in the community, their involvement with and assessment of the Southdown Project, and what had happened to them as adults. The interviews, with permission, were tape recorded and subsequently written up. Some took as little as a half an hour, others over two hours. It was a moving experience to meet again with former youngsters with whom I had been very close, often during difficult times. I was always made welcome and a number of the participants mooted the idea of a reunion which did take place at a later stage. As once again I walked the streets of Southdown, I met parents and other residents who had been involved in the Southdown Project. They too expressed an interest in my study and I later interviewed some of them as a kind of supplement to the main investigation.

I do not call this study 'research'. It had no control group of youngsters who did not attend the project, no comparisons with other and different projects. Its findings are based on the subjective opinions of those interviewed and on my personal interpretations. None the less, I hope what follows is of interest to practitioners, policy makers and all others concerned with the well-being of young people.

My thanks are due to Eric Adams of the Barrow Cadbury Trust who, not for the first time, expressed his backing for the grass roots work I have undertaken. Geoffrey Mann of Russell House Publishing Ltd has been encouraging about the book, partly because he is involved in youth work himself. The former Southdown team have always remained my friends: Jane Sellars kindly undertook some of the interviews: Jim Davis gave useful advice: Dave Wiles was always interested and he and Donna and their children kindly looked after me during my visits to Southdown. I am grateful to my son David Holman for statistical advice. Above all, my thanks go out to all the people we interviewed, most of whom appear in this book under pseudonyms. As I revisited the kids at the door, as I saw how they had grown and developed, then I was mightily pleased that I had been associated with them in the decade 1976–86.

Chapter Two

The Youngsters

Their Background

Of the 51 in the study group, 35 were males and 16 females. What was their background as youngsters? From what kind of families did they come? At the time they first made contact with the Southdown Project, 46 were living on the adjoining Southdown and Whiteway estates. Most were in Southdown itself and henceforth the term Southdown will be used to refer to both estates. Of the remaining five, one dwelt in another council estate about a mile away, one in a nearby village and three in a nearby area of private housing. Of the 46, all but four had spent all or most of their lives in the area. The four had moved in after living in another part of Bath or other towns in the West Country. This uniformity of residence was reinforced by the fact that 47 of the 51 youngsters lived in local authority accommodation. It seemed too that most of their parents were from Bath and surrounding areas. With two exceptions, all the youngsters were of white parents.

What of their family composition,

Table 1. – Types of Families in which the Youngsters Lived.

	No.	%
Lone mother	13	25
Lone father	5	10
Mother and stepfather	6	12
Both natural parents	27	53
Total	51	100

It can be seen from Table 1 that 18 children, that is 35%, were in lone parent families. The comparable figure for Britain as a whole in 1981 was 12%. A further six were with their mothers and a stepfather, so overall 24, that is 47% of the youngsters were not living with both their natural parents. All 24 concerned families where a partner had left, none were the result of single parents who had never had a settled partner. It should be added that some of these relationships broke up during the time the youngsters were involved with the Southdown Project. Thus they had experience in both a two-parent and a one-parent household.

Of the 38 present fathers and stepfathers, 12 were unemployed. Of the 26 in work, their occupations covered the following: engineer, driver, delivery man, joiner, postman, printer, proof-reader, wall builder, general builder, computer operator, security guard, taxi driver, handyman, caretaker, labourer. 23 of the mothers were in jobs, often part-time. One was a nurse and one a clerical worker but the predominant occupations were cleaners, dinner ladies, waitresses and shop assistants. The youngsters nearly all came from what were then called working class homes and lived in a working class location. None had affluent, professional parents.

Bath is a long way from the East End of London. The image of the former is that of a wealthy spa town while that of the latter is of low-incomed families joined by ties of kin and neighbourhood. But there is another, poorer Bath, especially on its council estates, just as there is another East End of London. Interestingly the study group youngsters of the late 1970s and early 1980s show something in common with the East Enders studied by Peter Willmott in the 1950s and 60s. Both tended to be from working class homes, to have parents on moderate or low incomes, to live in council houses and to have stayed in the same neighbourhood for some years, (Willmott, 1969, Chapter 1).

Vulnerable Youngsters

How likely were the study sample to experience social disadvantage, anti-social behaviour and personal distress as they grew older? Their background offers some clues for there are experiences and circumstances which predispose some children towards these adverse outcomes. In *Antisocial Behaviour by Young People*, Rutter, Giller and Hagell have made a comprehensive review of the relevant research. They summarise the 'long list of psychosocial risk factors' as 'broken homes, single parent families, teenage parents, family discord, abuse or neglect, coercive parenting, lack of supervision, family criminality, large family size, delinquent peer groups, poor schooling and living in a socially disorganised area' (1999, p 168). In a shorter review, Utting, Bright and Henricson draw upon longitudinal studies of young people to identify the factors most linked with juvenile delinquency,

(1993). They particularly refer to research by Wadsworth, Kolvin, and West and Farrington. Utting, has also reviewed research which examines what leads to social and emotional difficulties in young people (1995). Two other studies are of importance. One, by Bebbington and Miles studied a large sample of children who were received into public care (1989). The other, by Cockett and Tripp considered the effects on young people of their parents' separation or divorce (1994).

From these and other studies, the following vulnerability or 'at risk' factors emerge as of significance.

1. Low Income. Utting, Bright and Henricson concluded, 'Children from low-income, working class families are more likely to become delinquent than those from comfortable middle class homes', (1993, p 18). Similarly, those from homes characterised by poverty and from socially deprived locations are more likely to enter public care, to do badly at school, or to be unemployed.

2. Unsatisfactory Child Rearing. Parents who neglect their children, whose supervision is lax or erratic, whose discipline is too harsh, whose family relationships are marked by conflict, may well raise children who are not only more prone to offending but also to repeating the pattern of their own parents' behaviour.

3. School Difficulties. Unsatisfactory parenting is also associated with children who show disruptive behaviour at school, who truant, and who underachieve. In turn, these school difficulties are often associated with offending and poor employment.

4. Large Family Size. West found that children from large families, four or more children, were more likely to offend than those from smaller families, (1968, pp 73–74). Similarly, they do less well at school.

5. Disrupted and Lone Parent Families. The research by Cockett and Tripp indicated that children whose parents separated or divorced were more likely to report low self-esteem, difficulties with friendships, problems with school work, behavioural difficulties and health troubles. Further, following the disruptions, children may find it hard to adjust to step-parents and step-siblings. Utting, Bright and Henricson draw attention to the Oregon Youth Study which concluded that, 'Boys who had experienced divorce by the age of 10 were observed to exhibit more behavioural problems than children in intact families, but those living with a step-father were even more likely to be antisocial', (1993, p 19).

The academics Dennis and Erdos make a connection between lone mothers and delinquent boys and tend to blame the mothers for bringing them up without the discipline and model of a father, (1992). Utting, Bright and Henricson, while acknowledging a connection between single parenthood and offending, do not adopt the same condemnatory attitude towards single mothers and, indeed, assert that lone parenthood can be better for children than partners who constantly fight and argue.

The weight of evidence is that certain circumstances and experiences, particularly those listed above, do make children more vulnerable to adverse developments. However, some important qualifications must be made.

- Exposure to the vulnerability factors does not inevitably bring about disadvantageous outcomes. Some children endure them and thrive. For instance, most poor children do not become delinquent teenagers and criminal adults. It is just that experience of the 'at risk' factors makes them more likely to do so than those who do not experience them. None the less, it is also true that a number of children from the most favoured backgrounds and conditions will become offenders, do badly at school etc. It follows that it is just not possible to predict with complete accuracy how any individual child will turn out.

- Only a small number of children may react adversely to the vulnerability factors. For instance, in their study, Cockett and Tripp noted that most children subject to parental divorce or separation do *not* exhibit long-term difficulties and that only 'a significant minority of children encounter long-term problems', (1994, p 59). None the less, they are still more at risk than children not exposed to divorce and separation.

- The link between the vulnerability factors and adverse outcomes is not simple or direct. The children of lone parents may be more prone to behavioural problems. But lone parent families are also likely to be poor and to dwell in deprived areas and it may be the influence of these circumstances rather than having one parent which affects the children. Again, it is not just poverty in itself which makes children more anti-social, more delinquent, more disruptive at school. Wilson and Herbert established that long-term poverty makes parenting difficult which, in turn, can adversely affect children, (1978). In a much praised follow-up study of the children as they grew older, Wilson noted that:

  large family size and overcrowding lead to unsupervised play in streets and yards, and early severance of mother-child contact affects behavioural training. Children learn to adapt by developing techniques of aggression and withdrawal. (1987)

- Vulnerability factors often work in combination. This was made clear by Bebbington and Miles in their study of which children entered public care. Those most at risk were from one-parent families, were dependent upon Income Support, were of mixed racial origin and were in crowded homes, (1989).

For all the qualifications, there is no doubt that the experience of vulnerable factors puts children at risk at two main stages. Firstly, as youngsters, especially as teenagers, they are more likely to take prohibited drugs, to be taken into care, and underachieve at school and have difficulties in employment. Males are much more likely to commit offences. Females are more at risk of being lone, teenage mothers. Secondly, as adults, as Rutter, Giller and Hagell make clear, they are more prone to criminality, drug and alcohol abuse, unemployment and family breakups, (1999, chapter 10).

Following the above, the vulnerability factors can be grouped in five categories. Within each, questions were directed at the interviewees to see whether they had experienced them.

1. Money difficulties. Children reared in poverty or on low incomes are more vulnerable to the kind of problems already discussed. The study sample were asked whether their families had endured financial difficulties and shortages which stemmed from dependence upon welfare benefits or low wages.

2. Unsatisfactory Child Rearing. Children subjected to and made unhappy by parents who neglect their basic needs for food, affection, discipline and stimulation are also a vulnerable group. The study group were asked to talk about their childhood and then to rank it as 'happy', 'average', or 'unhappy'. Those saying they were unhappy were considered to have had unsatisfactory child rearing experiences.

3. Educational Difficulties. School problems are closely associated with later difficulties in teenage and adulthood. The study sample were asked to speak about their school life. They were graded as having school difficulties if they experienced at least two of the following: being disruptive at school, been a frequent bully, or being bullied, a persistent truant, and being suspended and/or expelled.

4. Large Families. Being part of a large family, usually measured as four or more children, is also recognised as a vulnerability factor.

5. Disrupted and Lone Parent Families. As shown above, children brought up by lone parents and in families where parents have separated and then linked up with other partners are more likely to face future difficulties than those who remain with their two natural parents. This information was easily ascertained as the study sample talked about their childhood.

Again, it must be said that the above factors do not necessarily affect children in a negative way. Certainly, large families may be happy families. But research indicates that these are the factors, usually in combination, which put some children at greater risk than others. They are not the only factors. For instance, there is some evidence that criminal parents are more likely to rear criminal children but to have asked interviewees about the criminal record of their parents might have given offence and so spoilt the rest of the interview. However, it was possible to collect material on five major areas. This material depended entirely on what the interviewees said. Unlike major research investigations, data could not be collected from their parents, schools, social workers etc. None the less, it was important to study what the former young people thought about their backgrounds and experiences. The information collected was shaped so that it applied to them in the years before they left school. Much of it, therefore, was around the period when the leaders were getting to know them which tended to be from the ages of 11–15 years. During this time, the Southdown Project kept some records and from these I gleaned that 20 of the study sample, nearly all boys, were in trouble with the police, although not always prosecuted. Further, that statutory social workers were concerned about eleven of the families from which the children came. However, I did not feed this into the measurement of vulnerability factors which depended only upon information supplied by the interviewees. On this basis the following information was assembled.

- 31 of the former youngsters had been in families with money shortages.
- 22 considered they had endured unhappy and unsatisfactory upbringings.
- 29 had faced persistent difficulties at school. It is worth mentioning that such difficulties were more marked amongst the boys than the girls, with 22 boys as against seven girls having school problems.
- 25 had been brought up in large families.
- 24 had had lengthy periods with lone parents or step-parents.

The youngsters probably most at risk were those who faced the largest number of vulnerability factors. These were distributed thus:

Table 2. – No. of Vulnerability Factors Amongst the Youngsters

	No.	%
0–1 (low risk)	15	29
2–3 (moderate risk)	16	31
4–5 (high risk)	20	39
Total	51	100

20 of the study sample could thus be considered highly at risk. Of these 14 were boys while six were girls, that is 40% of the boys and 38% of the girls. It can be concluded that the Southdown Project did draw in a considerable numbers of young-sters who were vulnerable to adverse developments both in their teen years and adulthood. At the same time, there were a core of youngsters at low risk as well as some in between. It was always the intention of the project to have a range of youngsters, to mix those with anti-social tendencies with those who were not. It must be added that the study group was made up of those who had regular and long-term contact with the leaders. In addition, the project served a larger number who just attended the clubs with, as far as was known, the great majority displaying no outstanding problems. The method of the project was thus to provide leisure facilities to a large number of youngsters who required no more than safe recreation while simultaneously seeing more of a core number which contained both those at risk and not at risk.

The mixture of the ordinary and the needy can be illustrated by citing the words of some of those interviewed in the various groups.

The low risk group

I had a good childhood. My parents were strict and good. They were hardworking, although sometimes money was tight. My grandparents lived near and I now live in their old house. I enjoyed life in the street, it was a bit like a soap. I never got into trouble at school and I liked it. I got two 'O' levels and four CSEs. I wanted to be a mechanical engineer but it didn't work out. But I got a fair job. (Matthew)

I had a safe and secure family. We lived in a cul-de-sac which was nice. My parents were really concerned about me. Dad was a chippy and joiner. I worked hard at school and enjoyed it. (Archie)

I had a happy childhood with good parents. I enjoyed school. (Ann)

I had a nice childhood. Our parents have stayed together whereas those of many of our friends have parted. We had a good upbringing. Mum did most of it because dad was abroad a lot but he was a good father, good fun. We lived here in Southdown since I was two so it was settled. I got on fine at school, I never skived. I enjoyed it, although I could have worked harder and achieved more. (Jill)

I had a very happy childhood. My parents did not have really good jobs but they managed. We never argued except over small things like keeping my bedroom clean. I liked school and was never in trouble. (Tanya)

My father left when I was born and I had no contact with him. but I had a very happy upbringing. My mother was left on her own but we never wanted for anything. I got on well with most of the kids at school, and finished up with seven CSEs. (Val)

I lived in a close community surrounded by kids of my own age. My parents looked after me well. But I did get in quite a bit of trouble at school, playing up the teachers, arguing with other kids. I was a bit of a rebel. (Thorpe)

I was brought up in a Roman Catholic home with my mum, dad, sister and brother. They were very strict and I had to be in on time. My parents were close and were there when I wanted them. (Agnes)

I had a normal working class upbringing. Dad worked in a factory and mum worked part-time as a cleaner. I did OK at school although I never liked sport. I did enough to get by. (Dylan)

I was adopted although I did not find out until I was 13. I've always had it in the back of my head about finding my real parents. But it didn't make much difference because I couldn't have wished for better parents. I was the only child so a bit spoilt. I didn't get on very well at school. I was always in trouble and suspended three times. (Syd)

The moderate and high risk groups

My dad left when I was seven. Later we had a stepfather and we got on pretty well. I gave my mum a lot of hassle. I wouldn't stay in. I used to jump out the window. Sometimes mum would pack her bags and say she was going. I didn't get on well at school, I was always in trouble. I couldn't handle anything, especially racist abuse. I got suspended. (Albert)

Dad worked long hours and was always out. He drank a lot. (Malcolm)

My mum was mentally ill. My parents split up and I lived with my dad. I did badly at school. I truanted, didn't do exams. I felt alone and started getting into trouble with the police. (Arnold)

My parents split up and I had a stepfather who drank heavily. I had to go to his club and stick up skittles five times a week. I was unhappy, always arguing with him. I felt lonely. I missed a lot of school because I was staying out so late at his club. I suffered from migraines a lot, then I started skiving off school and a social worker came round. (Saul)

I did not get on with my dad who used to beat me. When I was seven I went to a Home. I went back home but I got into trouble. I stayed off school and got expelled. (Roland)

My mum and dad split up when mum left. My dad brought us up. With five kids, dad out of work, we were poor. And we kids were always arguing. At school I got bullied a lot. I was always in trouble. I always seemed to be in the wrong. I skived at times. I can't read or write. (Wilf)

Our parents separated and our mum took up with a bloke who was alcoholic. She never understood what she was doing to us. Once we were so hungry that my brother and I mixed flour and water for something to eat. I hardly went to school. I just felt bored. (Anthea)

I didn't get on well with my mum. We were arguing all the time. I was cheeky. Then our parents split up. I used to skive off school. We used to go down to Bob's house and try to say it was a study day. I got suspended. (Thelma)

My mother and father were divorced when I was four. I rarely saw my father after that but later we did get together and that helped me a lot. Shortly after the divorce my brother was born. I never got on well with him. It always appeared to me when I was younger that he was the blue-eyed boy. If I ever wanted anything I had to work for it, if he wanted anything he got it. When we had arguments it was always my fault. It was very difficult for mum. She was on Income Support. At junior school, I had a personality clash with the head. There were lots of problems. I got accused of doing something by the headmistress. My mum fought my corner but I got the cane. I left the school for another junior school. I got on well at secondary school but I was lazy. I just didn't want it. I was always at the bottom of the class, bottom of the year. It wasn't until the last two years that I was offered subjects that I found interesting like engineering and motor mechanics. Outside of school, I was getting into trouble with petty pilfering. I had two paper rounds and if I saw something I liked I would pick it up and take it. I used to go into mum's purse and take money and spend it on silly things. I remember I stole some plasters from the school first aid kit when we had Jucos at Moorlands school. Bob found out and made me take them back. (George)

The background, the kinds of families they came from, and the vulnerability factors of the youngsters have now been established: 70 per cent of the youngsters possessed vulnerability factors which placed them at moderate to high risk. These were their circumstances and experiences when they came to the project. The next topics to be explored concern how they made contact with the Southdown Project and what kind of activities they attended.

Chapter Three

The Youngsters and the Project

How did the Southdown Project reach the youngsters? What services did it offer? What activities went on? What did the study group think of them? These are the main questions addressed in this chapter.

The Southdown Project, at its start, operated from Bob and Annette's house. When youngsters wanted youth clubs a search had to be made for a suitable venue. As explained, the first venue was Hallett's Studios, an old and draughty prefab which an artist used as his studio. He was pleased to receive some rent for its use. Unfortunately, the senior youth club users did some minor damage to the property and later there was a break-in for which members got blamed. The next hall was that of the Ascension church. Its advantages were that the facilities were spacious and the vicar co-operative. The disadvantages were that it was some way outside of Southdown, that a number of church members complained that the club was not serving the church's young people, that there was little storage space so that all the gear had to be taken down and returned after each gathering, and that the youngsters often came early and created a noise which disturbed neighbours. Next the clubs moved into the hall of St Barnabas' church which was within Southdown. The vicar was enthusiastic and, moreover, there was some green space outside which proved invaluable for games when the junior youth clubs became very crowded. The drawback was that the hall was periodically used by adult organisations, such as the drama club, which meant it was not always available. In between these times, the senior youth club often met at Bob's house. The Jucos club met at a school and a non-conformist church on the edge of Southdown. The Jucos was a Christian junior club linked to a national movement called Covenanters. The word Jucos was an abbreviation of Junior Covenanters. It had a Sunday morning meeting consisting of quizzes, a few games and a short talk and a club night in the week. Sometimes it also had Saturday morning activities while members could go to an annual camp held at West Runton in Norfolk. No pressure was put on youngsters to go to Jucos and all the other clubs had no explicit Christian content. After 1983, the Southdown Project had its own centre and all the varied youth clubs transferred to it.

Reaching the Youngsters

For six years the project had no permanent premises, no building with a notice board advertising the Southdown Project. How then did the study sample get drawn into the project? Some answers are given in the following table.

Table 3. – Contacting the Project

	No.	%
By friends	29	57
By leaders	15	29
By parents	5	10
By location	2	4
Total	51	100

The initial members of the senior youth club were likely to be drawn in through direct contact with Dave and Bob. Early on, the two leaders spent time walking the streets. They joined in football kickabouts, stood around in the evenings with the teenagers, and made sure that, when they met anyone, they introduced the project. Soon it became obvious that the young people could contact Bob and Dave at the house. After a short while, some met there to discuss the possibility of a club. Even after the clubs were established, the leaders made a point of knocking at the door of any family who moved into the area and inviting them to activities. In all, 15 of the former youngsters considered that the personal contact with the leaders was an important element in making them a part of the Southdown Project. The following quotations illustrate this point.

> *It was through Dave Wiles. He was a bit of a character. Then he settled down and came to talk to us in the streets and we got the club at Hallett's Studios.* (Ashley)

> *It was Dave Wiles. Then Bob came on the scene and we used to go down to his house.* (Matthew)

> *I was playing football and Bob Holman and his son joined in and told us about the project.* (John)

> *Bob used to come round the streets talking to everyone. That is how we met.* (Thelma)

> *We used to hang about the streets and in the garages. Then Bob approached us and I went to the senior club.* (Val)

Once the project was established with regular junior and senior clubs, youngsters were more likely to be invited by mates who were going. Sometimes they observed that their friends were attending the clubs and tagged along. The main reason given, covering 29 of the study group, for joining in with project activities was the influence of friends. Some of the youngsters put it as follows:

> *A friend said, 'Come down to Bob's house.' I started playing in the football team. Then I went to the clubs. Other kids in the street were going along.* (Arnold)

> *Other kids were joining. The first thing I went to was a trip to Alton Towers.* (Donald)

> *I moved into Southdown. Everyone seemed to be going and I went ever since.* (Saul)

> *I was taken along by some mates. They were going to the dinner time club at Bob's.* (Syd)

> *Friends used to hang about together and we went to the club at St Barnabas' hall.* (Jill)

> *My friend took me along to the Christmas party.* (Bella)

Five youngsters were introduced by their parents. Eric's mum was attending one of the mothers' groups and she told him about the clubs. Thorpe said, 'My mum started helping at the project and she took me along with her.' His mum had become a helper at one of the play schemes and it suited her to take Thorpe at the same time. An even smaller number, two, just knew the location of the project once the new centre was built and was open from morning to night. Wilf was an unemployed teenager when, as he put it, 'I just walked in. Soon I was there every day to play table tennis and pool.'

The Clubs and Holidays

The study sample was asked to look back some 12–23 years. Yet the passing years did not seem to dim their memories about the Southdown Project. In particular, almost all had vivid memories about the youth clubs, the outings, the sports and the holidays. The next chapter will discuss what benefit they gained from these activities. Here the aim is to catch something of the enjoyment they experienced.

Nearly all those interviewed had been regularly to at least one of the youth clubs. A distinction can be made between those who might be called founder members, that is, the teenagers who joined the first senior club, those who came in a few years later, probably starting at the junior clubs, and those who attended the Jucos. Some quotations from each follow.

The Founder Members

The club was first in Bob's house, in the living room. We used to sit on the stairs. It was comfortable and welcoming. We used to look forward to it. Then we went to Hallett's Studios. It was cold, blocked toilets, a hollow sound as people ran in and out. It sounds awful but it was fun and we looked forward to the next night. (Tanya)

The clubs started at Hallett's Studios. I ran the little tuck shop. We only had bits and pieces because in those days there was not a lot to spend on equipment. Then we had to take it back to Bob's afterwards. Then we had football and cricket. I looked forward to the matches and was disappointed if they were cancelled. It was the only chance we had of competing at a different level. (Matthew)

It wasn't like school where the teachers had a lot of authority. The clubs were very relaxed and the leaders made something for everybody. I liked the table tennis and games. But especially the music. Bob let us play records. (Jill)

We started at the Ascension church hall. Then we moved to St Barnabas. We had a good time, badminton, snooker on a table with most of the balls missing. Cricket I loved. I remember umpiring when Bob's son made a big appeal for a catch behind. I could see it flicked the pad so I gave it not out. Bob came up to me and said 'Nice decision.'

Junior Club Members

I started at St Barnabas' church hall. We had a cricket team, usually Thursday evenings at Odd Down. We had an annual race up Roundhill, I won it one year and I've still got the cup. We had great fun. I'm sorry I've grown up. I'd like to do it all again. (Sandy)

We had Monday Club in St Barnabas when we were raising money for the building. When it was up I went all the time to the centre. Before-school club and after-school club. I liked the knock-out tournaments–darts, table tennis, pool. Sometimes we had day trips and adventure days. (Saul)

We could do our own thing at the clubs–as long as we didn't wreck the place. We used to muck about with Dave and Jim–boxing them. We had a good laugh with Jane. It is so different now. There is so much that children can't do what we used to do. (Tyson)

Everyone on the estate used to go. There was table tennis, games, darts. It was really nice. (Ann)

I went mainly to the clubs once the centre was built. I could mix with those who were unemployed like me as well as the employed. Sometimes I did muck about just to get barred. But it was good. (Syd)

The Jucos Members

I went mainly to the Jucos. Everyone seemed to meet there for the games night. We played pool, table tennis, had a tuck shop, used to 'beat-up' the leaders. (Thorpe)

We were always doing something, meeting everyone, going on the trips. We used to go swimming at the Oasis in Swindon and stop for chips on the way back. Bob would go in and ask for 40 bags. (Albert)

I enjoyed going out. I remember going to an adventure playground, going across the ropes and down the slides. The slides were so steep, we were all saying, 'You do it first.' We went up to Rainbow Woods for the wide game. (Donald)

I went to Jucos on Sundays and then there were various things to do in the week. Club was in the school. I had a good time there. We built goal posts for three-a-side football. I went to Juco camp. I also went camping at Keswick with Bob and his family.

I've got a lot of fond memories of Jucos, going swimming at the Oasis. We had a lot of fun. It just seemed my kind of environment, I was like the other kids who went. I could communicate with them. The leaders were fun and friendly. Eric was one of the kids who then became a helper and we had a lot of fun together. Years later, when I was homeless, I met him again at the hostel where he was working. (George)

The pattern became for the youth clubs to close down during the school's summer vacations and to be replaced by play schemes and residential holidays. The senior youth club started with holidays at Pontin's 'hi-de-hi' style holiday camp at Filey. The Jucos went every August to their under canvas camp at West Runton. As time went on, other locations became Bournemouth, where a children's home allowed us to camp in its grounds; Plymouth, where a similar facility was provided by a teachers' training college; Dartmoor, where a local church made the arrangements; and George-ham in North Devon where we took over a large country house. In addition, a friend of mine, Laurie Laken, often took small groups of youngsters to the Isle of Dogs in East London where he worked as a qualified trampoline and table tennis coach.

44 of the study sample had been on at least one holiday with the Southdown Project. The leaders knew that the holidays did sometimes encounter difficulties. The youngsters' aggressive behaviour at the first Filey led to a 'last warning' from the officials. Arguments sometimes broke out between members. At Plymouth, the campers were accused of breaking into the college bar. One of the West Runton camps endured a week of rain so heavy that the marquee tent collapsed under the weight of water. The leaders also knew that overall they were very successful with both youngsters and leaders wanting to go again and again. Certainly, the former youngsters who were interviewed had no trouble in remembering the holidays and all expressed their appreciation. Some typical comments are:

> *In 1977, I went to Filey. We went in Dave's old Commer van, 50 miles an hour if it was down hill and the wind behind you. Filey was cold but fun. I remember Bob taking us to York for the day.* (Ashley)

> *We went to Filey. There were clangers and whistles to get you up. I remember going out for the day to Scarborough where we went on a speed boat and got a soaking. It was really good fun. It took so long to get home in the mini bus with Bob driving.* (Tanya)

> *I went three times to the Juco camp. I liked playing on the sand dunes. We went to the woods for the wide game where you had to get other people's arm bands. I enjoyed making kites–I lost three of them. While I was at one camp in 1986, my dad died. Bob did not tell me then but I knew, it was instinct. He told me when we got back.* (Donald)

> *The Juco camps were great. I loved the canoes and crabbing on the pier. I've still got the photos.* (George)

> *The Jucos camp at West Runton was brilliant. There was so much fun, so many activities. We would go out in the day then have a book read to us at night.* (Thorpe)

> *We had a good laugh at camp. It was very well laid back. Everyone was happy with each other. It went smoothly. Jim was my tent officer.* (Lex)

> *We went to St George's in Devon and then Jane took the girls camping at Bournemouth. I enjoyed the swimming and canoes.* (Ann)

I went camping at least three times. We camped in the grounds of a children's home in a field with horses. That was good fun. Then to St George's, the big house next to the churchyard. The boys used to be on the graves and suddenly sit up and frighten us to death. We had a riot there. (Jill)

I remember being at the beach at night and we ran away from Bob and Dave, and Dave fell over and twisted his ankle and the tide was coming in. Then one girl ran in to the sea threatening to drown herself because of a boy. (Val)

Until the new centre was erected, the clubs were held in sometimes cold, sometimes overcrowded premises. The holidays were hardly luxurious. No hotels, no trips abroad. More usual was camping in a field. But the youngsters came. One reason was that the Southdown Project was their only option since the estate was characterised by a lack of youth facilities. Only three youngsters went to any other youth organisation, with two going to a Sunday School and one to a gym club outside the area.

For 48 the project was their only youth outlet. Similarly, a number mentioned that the Southdown Project gave them their only holidays since their own families never went and they could not afford the school trips. If nothing else, the clubs and holidays plugged a gap.

The House

Bob and Annette's house was the starting venue of the project. Within the first month, teenagers were meeting there to plan the youth club and, indeed, the club sometimes met there. Once the halls were obtained, it might have been anticipated that the use of the house would decline. Not so. Youngsters would frequently drop in to ask what was happening, when was the next trip and so on. A core of members participated in loading the gear into the transport prior to taking it to the hall and then would return it – followed by a late night cup of coffee in the kitchen. Gradually, some of the teenagers began to meet in the greenhouse, an old lean-to on the side of the house. It contained nothing but a few old chairs and a table but it proved popular. Bob and Annette – and Dave who had taken up digs in the house – would provide coffee and biscuits and then leave the youngsters alone. During the summer, they would sit and play on the patio outside. Later, after Jane Sellars and Jim Davis joined the project, a small lunch club started in the house at which soup, rolls and coffee were provided at a modest price. One of its objectives was to ensure that the youngsters went back to school after lunch and Jim would usually drive them there in the minibus. On Sundays Bob and his family, Dave and Jim usually went to a small chapel in a nearby village. It was organised by John Davis, Jim's dad, who ran a paper and rags salvage yard. He was a very humble man. I recall him saying, 'I'm even below the dustman, I take the stuff he won't.' He had restored the derelict chapel and led informal and often amusing services. His down-to-earth and informal style appealed to some who would have been uncomfortable in more orthodox churches. Some of the youngsters also started to attend and, as numbers grew, the evening would start with a cup of tea in the greenhouse, proceed with the minibus taking them to the service, and end with a run to the local chippie.

48 of the study group recalled activities in the house, and they looked back fondly at it.

> *Annette often let us into the house. At the time you don't think about it but the way she let us use her home–well, I can't describe it. Sometimes the boys were not very respectful of the home but Bob gave them free range and then they respected him.* (Tanya)

> *We played cards for hours. One of the boys strummed his guitar. We talked about music and pop groups.* (Joanna)

> *I was almost a resident. We were all together. Bob made us feel welcome.* (Tilly)

> *The greenhouse was somewhere to go. We played cards and drank coffee. We never did anything wrong like taking drugs there.* (Thelma)

> *In the daytime the house was open for people suspended from school. In the evening we were in the greenhouse. Bob's house was where everybody went.* (Bella)

> *I still think of it when I drive past the house. I went round once on a Sunday afternoon and we were breaking up wood for a bonfire. I jumped on a piece of wood which came up and split my lip open and I had to go to hospital.* (Wynn)

> *We played in the garden. Bob's house was full of kids and we sat in the greenhouse.* (Albert)

> *I liked climbing the tree in Bob's garden and playing the electronic boxing game in the house.* (Saul)

> *I used to go and play swing ball in the garden. Then we did a sponsored 'stay-awake' in the greenhouse. We were always hanging about there. I knew Bob's son, I was in his class. A whole crowd of us were in the greenhouse.* (Dan)

The use of the house by so many young people also served to build and cement relationships between them and the leaders. Some perceived that, should they need help with personal difficulties, then there were adults whom they could trust and a place where they could meet privately. As will be discussed later, 33 did seek individual help. The youngsters who were associated with the project thus attended clubs, went on outings and holidays, were likely to know Bob and Annette's house, and could avail themselves of individual help from the leaders. The next question is, what effect did all this have on their lives?

Chapter Four

How Did They Turn Out?

To date, the book has described how the Southdown Project was set up, what was the background of the youngsters, how many vulnerability factors they had, how the project contacted them and what kind of activities they attended. From what the 51 in the study sample said, there is little doubt that they enjoyed the clubs, the trips, and the holidays. Most felt free to drop into the house and to form relationships with the leaders. So what happened to them? How did they turn out? The question will be answered in two stages. First, a look will be directed at how they were doing in their older teenage years of 16–19. Second, how they turned out in adulthood, that is from 20 upwards.

The Teenagers

When the project started, it initially drew in a core of secondary school youngsters aged 13–15 years. Later it opened up to juniors and had clubs for 9–12 year olds. The play schemes catered for even younger ones. It follows that the leaders knew some children from a much earlier age and so may have had a greater influence over them. In the analysis which follows, no distinctions will be made on the basis of how long they were known.

What factors should be used to assess how they performed in their later teenage years from 16–19? The ones picked stem from the adverse outcomes which have already been shown to be linked with vulnerability factors. Unsatisfactory teenage behaviour was categorised as the following:

- Obtaining no educational qualifications at school.
- Being brought (and convicted) before the court at least five times or given a custodial sentence.
- Leaving home following disagreements with parents or being received into public care.
- Being unemployed for a total of at least six months.
- Regularly taking hard drugs or drinking alcohol excessively.

It might be countered that the emphasis is on negative factors, on how badly they did. Not so. Later sections will give attention to those who succeeded at school and work and to those who became helpers at the project.

- 24 failed to obtain any educational qualifications from school, indeed several left before they even took their final examinations. This was the one area of poor performance where the proportion of girls was as high as the boys.

- seven (all boys), of the total were convicted of an offence at least five times during these years, although none were given a custodial sentence. Another nine, including two girls, were in court less than five times. An example of one who went at least five times was Wilf who said, 'I got done for shoplifting and burglary several times. I got fines and conditional discharges. I didn't go to prison then.'

- nine experienced lengthy spells of unemployment. Some, like Eric, found it difficult to obtain a post after leaving government work schemes. George, by contrast, went through nine different jobs from which he was laid off or dismissed and then experienced a few weeks or months unemployment until he talked his way into another one.

- four of the youngsters admitted that they were taking hard drugs during the years 16–19. Another five said they often took soft drugs. Amongst these were three who added that they were also drinking quite heavily. George said, 'I was into cannabis. I was drinking a lot to the point where I went from work straight into the pub and sometimes was carried out.'

- five of the study sample left their homes following arguments with their parents. For instance, Saul said, 'I left home at 16 and moved in with my brother for a bit. I slept rough for a couple of nights and then got a live-in job at a pub.' George also had a spell sleeping in a car. Only one of the teenagers, however, went into public care. Anthea had an unhappy relationship with her step-dad which contributed to her withdrawal and need to escape. She explained, 'It was because of my truancy. I went to court and was put into care and sent to a children's home.'

Not recorded within the above figures but worth mentioning is that two of the girls had babies at the age of 16 and became young single mothers.

If the display of only 0–1 of the above factors is taken to indicate 'satisfactory' behaviour during the upper teenage years, 2–3 factors seen as 'cause for concern' and 4–5 factors as 'unsatisfactory', then the following table can be presented.

Table 4. – Later Teenage Behaviour

	No.	%
0–1 factors Satisfactory	39	76
1–2 factors Cause for concern	11	22
4–5 factors Unsatisfactory	1	2
Total	51	100

The majority of youngsters, 39, had satisfactory years between the ages of 16–19. 11 showed sufficient factors to be a matter for concern while only one could be seen as highly unsatisfactory. The latter was a youngster who gave up on school and got heavily into crime, hard drug abuse and dealing (in percentage terms 76 per cent displayed satisfactory behaviour while 24 per cent did not).

These outcomes are better than might have been anticipated from the distribution of vulnerability factors in which 20 were considered at high risk, 16 at moderate risk, and only 15 at low risk. The behaviour outcome factors and the vulnerability factors can be shown together in truncated form in the following table.

Table 5. – Relationship between Behaviour Outcomes and Vulnerability Factors

	Teenage behaviour factors	
Vulnerability factors	0–1 factor Satisfactory	4–5 factors Unsatisfactory and cause for concern
0–1 factors Low risk	14	1
2–5 factors Moderate and high risk	25	11

The trend is clear. Youngsters with 0–1 risk factors were more likely than others to achieve satisfactory outcomes. Those with moderate and high risk factors were more likely to be a cause for concern or to have an unsatisfactory outcome. (Using the *Fischer's Exact Test* and dividing the vulnerability factors at 0–2 and 3–5, the association is statistically significant.) But the interesting point is that so many moderate and high risk youngsters actually had satisfactory outcomes. 25 bucked the anticipated trend. For instance, Arnold was raised by a lone father in a home where he felt unhappy, at school he was disruptive and frequently absent, and in the streets he showed tendencies towards crime and vandalism. Yet subsequently the only negative outcome seemed to be leaving school with no qualifications. Thelma came from a large, low-incomed family where she was distressed by the breakup of her parents marriage while her troubled career at school resulted in suspensions. Yet, apart from one court appearance and obtaining no qualifications, she soon settled down into a useful and satisfying job and into a stable lifestyle. Again, it is worth saying that, despite the high number of boys who were in trouble with the police in their early teens and before, and despite the involvement of statutory social workers with 11 of the families, no older teenagers were sentenced to penal custody and only one was received into public care. Clearly something had helped them change course.

The Adults

The study group are no longer teenagers, How are they now? What has happened to them between the ages of 20 and the present? This section will concentrate on the following.

1. **Their Current Profile.** The present location, housing tenure, family situations and leisure pursuits will be drawn together to give an up-to-date profile of the study group.

2. **Adult Life Satisfactions.** In an earlier chapter, it was shown that not many of the youngsters were born into or brought up with social and economic advantages. Indeed, most of them were handicapped by 'at risk' factors that made them vulnerable to crime, unemployment, unhappy relationships, etc. It will be shown how many experienced as adults the following unsatisfactory factors:

   - Severe unemployment, that is out of work for a total of 12 months.
   - Criminal behaviour as revealed in three convictions (apart from minor vehicle offences) and/or a prison sentence or an alternative to prison sentence.
   - Drug or alcohol abuse as seen in the taking of prohibited hard drugs or heavy drinking over several years.

- Severe debt. Of course many people are in acceptable debt and, for instance, are regularly paying a mortgage. Here severe debt is seen as having difficulties in repaying debts of over £100. These might apply to debts with legal firms such as catalogues or illegal ones such as loan sharks.

- Broken family relationships, seen as the breaking up of a relationship which involved not just a partner but also children.

Factors are then rated on a satisfaction scale as follows:

0–1 factors = satisfactory adult lives

2–3 factors = unsatisfactory adult lives

4–5 factors = very unsatisfactory adult lives.

In short, adults who were mainly free from unemployment, criminality, drink or drug abuse, large debts and severe broken relationships were rated as having satisfactory lives. Those whose lives were characterised by them were rated as unsatisfactory or very unsatisfactory. Of course, these are not the only experiences and behaviours which make up satisfactory and unsatisfactory lives. But they are important ones and they are ones about which the interviewer could ask straightforward questions.

3. **Youth Work Involvement.** It emerged that many of the study group had pursued an interest in youth work.

4. **Their Attitude to Christianity.** As some of the youngsters had attended a Christian club and others gone to a local church, it was felt to be of interest to discover whether the project had had a lasting Christian influence upon them.

Their current profile

Where are they now? Most of the study group are still in or very near to Southdown. Of the 51 in the study group, 28 were living in the Southdown/Whiteway area. 14 resided in some other part of Bath while a further seven were within ten miles of the city. Only two were living over 100 miles away. Their close identification with the area was also seen in that numbers had partners who also originated from Bath.

As noted earlier, the majority of the group, 47 had been brought up in council accommodation. By 1999, 28 were in council property (with 22 being tenants while another six lived with their parents). 21 were owner occupiers and it is worth noting that ten of these were in the process of buying their former council homes. Just two were in privately rented flats.

Table 6. – Family Composition of the Study Group

Types of Families	No.	%
With partner and own children	30	58
With partner and no children	5	10
With partner and stepchildren	4	8
Lone parent with own children	3	6
Living with own parents	6	12
Living alone	3	6
Total	51	100

(Included in the six living with their own parents were three men who were separated from their partners and children. The other three were childless. Amongst the three living alone was one man who was apart from his wife and children.)

It can be seen from Table 6 that 30 were with partners by whom they had children. Another five were in relationships with partners with no children. So by far the majority of the former youngsters appear to be in stable two-partner relationships with only four in step-parent situations and only three lone parents. This is not to imply that step or lone parent settings are necessarily inferior. For instance, two of the Southdown youngsters were childhood sweethearts who married and had a baby. The husband was an original member of the youth club, a brilliant footballer, a popular resident. Unfortunately, after a long illness, he died of cancer. His wife took time to come to terms with her own grief and to help her son through the trauma. Later she remarried happily and has had two further children. Despite such unavoidable cases, it is usually recognised that it is an advantage for children to be brought up by both their natural parents. This was happening for the majority of the children of the study group. Indeed, to date, more are enjoying this stability than their own parents did, for it will be recalled that 24 of the study group had lived in lone parent or step-parent families. However, it should be explained that some had reached their present stable positions after the breakup of earlier relationships. The numbers who had experienced serious broken relationships will be given in the next section.

Family life was central to most of the study group as can be illustrated in responses to a question about their hopes for the future. Some hoped for better careers and more money – 'to win the lottery'. However, this was usually in the context of wanting the best for their children. Some typical responses were as follows:

> *To carry on as we are. We are a happy family. My mum's down the road. My brothers and sister are all within touching distance. I am close to them and we all help each other. We are all bound together.* (Sandy)

> *Not get into debt. To go on as we are. To look after our three kids. I want to know where they are all the time. I don't want them to be like me. My wife says I am a good dad, perhaps too protective.* (Arnold)

> *I've got it. I'm married. I've settled down. I've got kids. I've got somewhere to live. We get a holiday every year. I would like a bit extra money.* (Mal)

> *Bring our own children up. I've thought about doing fostering. I want to help children.* (Ann)

> *To have another transplant operation. I was born with an illness which kills kidneys. I had a transplant which lasted three years then I was on dialysis for two years then another transplant. That failed and now I am back on dialysis. It makes me very tired and I feel guilty with our adopted daughter because she says 'Come and play' and I haven't got the energy. So I want another transplant and to carry on with our happy marriage.* (Joanna)

> *We've brought up four children. Now I want to be a trained staff nurse. I am due to start a four year degree course in nursing.* (Bella)

> *When I was young I longed to have a mum and a dad and a fire. I want my children to have a better life than me. I want my marriage to last. I want to get educated and I am taking two 'O' levels.* (Anthea)

> *I want to watch my kids grow up. Then I'd like to get a better job, perhaps as an ambulance driver or nurse.* (Rebecca)

Apart from family life and jobs, what else did the study group do? They were asked about their leisure activities.

Table 7. – The Main Regular Leisure Interest

	No.	%
Participating in sport	28	55
Social club	9	18
Visiting relatives	3	6
Church activities	2	4
Others	3	6
No time	6	12
Total	51	100

Being in their late 20s and 30s, 28 still pursued an active involvement in sport. They included 11 football players while others did weightlifting, golf, pool, gymnastics, running, archery, tennis and motto cross. One weightlifter was dedicated to his sport and had become the divisional champion in his class and rated No. 18 in Britain. Dedication of another kind was displayed by two who gave much time to church activities. One used puppets in schools and a mandolin in pubs as part of a Christian ministry. Another (and his wife) had become active churchgoers and took on voluntary cleaning and grass-cutting duties at the church. Nine were regular attendees at a social club where they played skittles, enjoyed a drink and mixed with their friends. Six said they were too busy with their jobs and children to have any leisure time.

The profile that emerges is that of youngish adults who have not moved far from their places of origin, who identify closely with their neighbourhoods, who dwell in modest homes, whether privately owned or rented from the council, who place great importance on the upbringing of their children yet who also enjoy a regular leisure pursuit. Of course, there were exceptions but the overall finding is of a settled and stable group. However, this point had taken some years to reach. The question remains, how satisfactory had their lives been?

Adult life satisfactions

- Unemployment and Work

Paid employment is of enormous importance in our society. It is both a means of status and a means of income. Unemployment is not only associated with poverty but also with ill-health, social isolation and low self-esteem. It is important, therefore, to discover how the study sample fared in regard to work.

At the time of the interviews, 27 of the 35 men were in full-time jobs, two were in part-time posts, one was a full-time student and five were unemployed. Amongst the 16 women, seven were looking after their children full-time, six combined child care with part-time work, and three worked full-time. What kind of work did they do or had they done? Information was sought on their main post (even if they were not doing it at the time of interview). Their jobs can be classified as follows.

Three, all men, were in senior management or consultant positions responsible for a large organisation with scores of employees.

Three, all women, were, or had been, in supervisory positions overseeing up to a dozen employees.

12 were in posts that had required considerable training and examinations. Examples are electrician, stone mason, computer operator, dental technician, wood machinist.

Six were in welfare posts including youth worker, nurse and home care worker.

26 were in posts which had required less training such as bin men, gardeners, building labourers, milkmen, lorry drivers, bar workers, clerical staff, domestic cleaners, catering staff, waitresses, shop assistants.

One was self-employed running a thriving window cleaning business.

Despite the low educational attainments of many of the study sample, the majority of the former young people obtained regular employment as adults. Although the 1980s were nationally a time of growing unemployment, Bath was a place which suffered less than most. Indeed, some of the 51 seemed to leave and obtain new jobs with some ease, although many appeared to be in low-paid posts. Certainly work was important to them and the following quotations give some idea of their experiences.

After school I went on a youth training scheme as a milkman. Later I passed the driving test and got the job and stayed for three years. I then went to Roman Glass for three years and when I got bored with being inside all the time I went back to being a milkman. I was unemployed for a bit, did odd jobs, worked in a yoghurt factory and now I deliver newspapers. (Sandy)

I was an apprentice chippy for a few months before moving to a shop. I worked for a pub for a few years and then had several jobs, one was flat roofing. Now I am a fork lift driver. I worked for a month at a holiday camp as an entertainer and that is what I'd like to get into to. (Saul)

You just got to keep looking for a job or you get your money stopped. But you go for five jobs a week and don't get them. It's a waste of time. Being dyslexic doesn't help. (Donald)

When I left school I soon got a good job as a glazier and I was there five years. I then moved on to another glazier in Bristol until I was laid off when I was 24. I haven't really worked since then, apart from bits and pieces. I've been out of work for five to six years. (Tyson)

I didn't do well at school and, when I left, I worked in a chip shop. I'd always wanted to be a carpenter and I got an apprenticeship at a cabinet makers but after a year it folded, although I was able to stay on at college. I then got a job in Bristol and have been there six years. I'm a qualified wood machinist, mainly making kitchens. (Thorpe)

I got a job straight away in computers at the Ministry of Defence and soon got temporary promotion. After five years I left to work for a company which had contracts with MOD. I moved with them to London for three years and then in 1998 I took another job in Bristol as a PC Technology Engineer. It is well paid but I aim to move on to be a self-employed consultant. (Seb)

For years I didn't have a settled job because I was into drugs and I had a bad car accident and lost the sight of one eye. When I was 22, I started cleaning windows and the Prince's Trust bought me a van. I started small and it's got busier and busier. It has been very successful and now I employ a helper. I'm proud of it. Now I want to expand in to the jewellery business in off-street trading. I'll still do the window cleaning with my partner looking after the jewellery. We can buy cheap and sell for about £5. Anyone can do anything if they set their mind to it. (Syd)

I went to a shoe shop on a youth opportunity scheme and later the manager took me on permanent. After two years he moved to another branch and wanted me to go. I didn't want to leave home and I did not get on great with the new manager. I got a job in the kitchens at the university and stayed there until I was pregnant. (Joanna)

I did a YTS job in an old people's home but I was too young and didn't like it. I worked for a while in a records shop. Then I trained as an electrician at Bath Tech and became a qualified electrician. I worked at that until I had children. (Bella)

I left school at 15. My mum had remarried again. I worked in a factory. Then I got a job as a washer-up in a restaurant and worked my way up to be chef. I made good friends with the people who worked there and met my husband. Lots of interesting people came in and it was a turning point for me. I decided I could be like them. (Anthea)

I worked in a shop. Then I became a dental nurse until I got married. When my children were 3 months and a year, I got a little cleaning job. Amazingly it was at the Southdown Project and it suited because I could take the baby with me. Later I was a dinner lady at Southdown Junior School. A friend asked me to work in the old people's home, a council home. The first time I went I thought, 'Oh what a smell, I can't work here.' Then I loved it. I had found my niche with the elderly. It was always temporary so when I saw an advert for a full-time Home Care job with the Social Services Department I got that. You are told who to visit and what to do. You bath people, give them tablets, Hoover, all different age groups. I really enjoy it. (Tanya)

So how many did experience long periods of unemployment. Ten men from the study sample had experienced periods out of work which totalled over 12 months. However, in three of these cases, the unemployment was due to serious accidents or illness. Amongst those 'available for work,' the unemployment was seven men. Interestingly, the study group had less unemployment as adults than as older teenagers. The majority of men and women in the study sample did find regular work and, as shown above, gained satisfactions from their jobs. True, many of the jobs were low-paid and, particularly amongst the women, were part-time. But the majority certainly embraced the work ethic.

- Criminality

12, all men, were convicted of an offence in adulthood. Five of these were for relatively minor matters such as speeding, no car taxation disc, drunk and disorderly. The remaining seven had the following offences and punishments. It must be added that these sentences sometimes followed previous offences for which lesser punishments had been given.

A community service order, served with the Roundhill Centre (as the South-down Project was later called), for burglary.

Two sentences of six months custody for breaking into cars.

Two short-term prison sentences for burglary.

18 months prison for participating in a post office robbery.

15 months in prison for receiving stolen goods.

A short prison sentence for the non-payment of fines following offences involving a stolen car.

Two years probation for stealing to feed a drug habit.

These seven from the study sample, (this is 20% of all the men), were marked as having a severe problem with criminality, although it is fair to add that only one had received the above sentence within the previous three years. Two examples are now given:

> *I went through a very bad patch. My mother had thrown me out of home again because I was sitting around not doing anything to get a job. I had to go to the hostel for the homeless where I met up with Eric whom I had known in the Jucos, he was on the staff there. I got into cannabis. I split up with my girlfriend which was the last straw. I hit rock bottom and tried overdosing. I went to court on suspicion of handling stolen goods and for having a stolen car. I could not pay the fines and that was why I went to prison.* (George)

> *I was unemployed, taking drugs and drink. When I was 21, I was sentenced to 15 months imprisonment for receiving.* (Wilf)

- Drug/Alcohol Abuse.

Eight men acknowledge that they had drunk heavily and/or taken prohibited drugs over a longish period. Two examples of what they said are as follows:

> *When I was 18, I used cannabis and drank a lot. I got fined for being drunk and disorderly. Later I earned good money on the building sites. I was on my own and all I could do was drink. Then I met my wife and she has sorted me out. We've got kids and I can't afford to drink.* (Mal)

> *I got into smoking dope, then speed, then crack, very, very heavily for about three years. I was having to steal about £40 a day to pay for it. I stole a cheque book. I hardly ever went home. I was dossing around. Then I got put on two years probation.* (Syd)

Syd was the only one to get into hard drugs. At the time of the interview, he had been drug free for some years. Five of the seven heavy drinkers had also broken the habit – usually after settling down with a partner and having children.

- Severe Debt.

A number of those interviewed acknowledged that they were often behind in payments to the tune of a few pounds. However, only three of the study sample were in serious debt. One owed £1,300. Another, whose story is given in the next chapter, had prolonged debts which led him being taken to court.

- Broken Family Relationships.

15 of the study group, ten men and five women, had endured separation from partners which caused them much emotional pain. 11 of these breakups, seven men and four women, also involved children and it is these ones which are rated as severe broken relationships. Two of the men had separated from two previous partners leaving children with both of them. Here is what three others, the first a man, the other two women, said:

> *I married at 17 to an older woman in the street who had two children. We had another one. The marriage led to arguments and violence in front of the kids. After seven years, it was better that I left. I now live with someone else but I still see my daughter.* (Tyson)

> *When I was 18, I got married. It was an awful relationship. He took to drinking and used to hit me. We had to get the police a couple of times. I got out with the children. I felt ashamed as if it was my fault. Since then I've married again. I've never been so happy as in the last couple of years.* (Rebecca)

> *I married very young and was soon a mother. My husband turned out to be horrible because of his drinking. Then I married again. I had another child. That failed again. Now I bring up the children on my own–although I have a partner who does not live with me.* (Joy)

The overall satisfactory ratings of the adult lives can be seen in the following table:

Table 8. – Adult Satisfactory Factors

	No.	%
0–1 factors		
Satisfactory adult lives	44	86
2–3 factors		
Unsatisfactory adult lives	6	12
4–5 factors		
Very unsatisfactory adult lives	1	2
Total	51	100

44 of the study sample were rated as living satisfactory adult lives. The great majority were free of unemployment, crime, drink or drug abuse and debt. Most were in stable relationships and looking after their own children. Only seven could be said to have endured unsatisfactory or very unsatisfactory lives. The one person rated as very unsatisfactory had experienced unemployment, had been to prison, had drunk heavily and was in debt. But, at the time of the interview, even he had settled down with a partner and children. (In percentage terms, 86 per cent were having satisfactory adult lives while only 14 per cent were not).

The outcomes are much better than might have been predicted from the disadvantages faced by many of the study group in their childhood when high numbers were in large, low incomed and often disrupted families, considered themselves unhappy and were soon showing problems at school. The relationship between the adult outcomes and the 'at risk' factors is shown below.

Table 9. – Relationship between Adult Outcomes and Vulnerability Factors

	Adult behavioural outcomes	
	0–1 factors	2–5 factors
	Satisfactory lives	Unsatisfactory and
Vulnerability factors		very unsatisfactory lives
0–1 factors	13	2
Low risk		
2–5 factors	31	5
Moderate to high risk		

It can be seen, not surprisingly, that those with a small number of vulnerability or 'at risk' factors did have satisfactory lives, with just two exceptions. Those with a higher number of vulnerability factors did have more chance of living unsatisfactory lives. However, the association is not statistically significant. The important finding is that most did not live up to the gloomy expectations. They did not go down the paths that led to social mal-behaviour. Three examples can illustrate the point.

1. One boy was a member of a large family brought up by a lone mother in poverty. He did badly at school and engaged in petty delinquency. Yet as an adult, he has stayed in jobs, kept clear of criminality and settled down in a stable relationship.

2. A girl lived with her mother and a violent, unemployed stepfather who spent much of their meagre income on drink. She truanted from school and gained no qualifications. She spent a few months in public care. As an adult she secured regular if low-paid employment, studied in her spare time, and now has two children within a happy marriage. She says she is determined that their marriage will last.

3. Another boy experienced the departure of his father when he was young. His mum struggled to bring him up on a low income. As a youngster he was wild and in frequent trouble at school. As an adult, he did serve a prison sentence but otherwise has been in jobs, has no drug or drink problems, no severe debts and is bringing up his son with his partner.

It was mentioned that the measure of life satisfaction might be criticised for emphasising negative factors, namely that it consisted of not being unemployed, not being convicted of crime and so on. So, in addition, the study sample were asked to rate their current happiness position as either happy, average or unhappy. 38 considered that they were happy, 13 thought they were average and none saw themselves as unhappy. Considering that some had endured an unhappy childhood, matters had improved. A number, when making their rating, added a comment. Some telling examples are as follows:

I've grown up and we are now stable. I haven't got a lot but I've got a home, three fabulous kids and a fabulous wife. The children are happy and we enjoy spending time with them. (George)

I am much happier than I was. The ways I react have changed. I think. I am a more sympathetic person than I was, I can control my behaviour a lot better and I don't let things get to me so much. (Eric)

I've got there. There was a time at work when I felt, 'I can't be bothered'.

But you've got to. At the end of the week when your wages go in the bank, you're glad. (Saul)

I've dragged myself up. I've seen the other side and you realise you don't have to be like that. (Anthea)

Both the statistics and the interviews reveal a heartening picture. They show that young people who start life with the kind of disadvantages that could put them on the track for crime, unemployment and social distress can turn the tables. Those from broken families do not have to repeat the pattern. Those with parents who were unemployed do find work. Those who were juvenile delinquents can break the habit. The chapter which follows will show this in more detail by some case examples of youngsters who struggled against the odds into adulthood. But, before that, two other aspects of adult life must be raised.

Involvement in youth work

The interview with the study sample included a question about any voluntary work they had undertaken. 25 had participated. Their activities included being a school governor, a committee member of a pro-motor bike organisation, raising money for Water Aid and helping children to read at school. But the majority, 21 named volunteering for youth work, particularly with the Southdown Project (some had undertaken youth work and also some other form of voluntary action).

It emerged that a major feature of the study sample was the number who had taken up youth work. All had started as volunteers but in some cases had gone on to be paid sessional staff and full-time workers.

For five the involvement was no more than helping out regularly at the junior clubs when they were aged 15 and over. One said:

I was a junior leader at the Jucos club. I went to the club nights and saw that the kids were alright and on Sunday I helped at the meetings. It made me nervous to get up and speak but it built up my character. I also went to the camp as a junior officer. That was hard work and good fun. It was great to meet all the other people there. (Malcolm)

Another five had more formal involvement. One served his Community Service Order with the project. Two were sent by their schools on work experience placements. Another worked in the clubs as his Youth Opportunities Placement. He stated, 'I did everything from 9 am in the morning. It was interesting to see what everybody actually did. I saw both sides of the question. I became associated with the leaders and, at the clubs, the kids used to jump on me.' (Mal) During his placement, he was expected to report on time, participate in the team meetings, attend the clubs, and to take on specific responsibilities like running the cafe. At the end of the period, he received a positive evaluation. Another was one of the early members of the senior club who soon married and had children. She then participated in the planning and running of the summer play schemes where she proved an able leader, particularly good at stimulating craft activities amongst the younger children. She remembered, 'It was brilliant because I could take my children with me'. (Tanya)

Seven of the young people (some of whom had also helped out at the junior clubs) went on to lead clubs once they were over the age of 18. They had benefited from the project's own youth training scheme designed by Dave Wiles with the aid of Ray Jones (as explained in Chapter Six). Those who satisfactorily completed the course were awarded the Southdown Youth Training Certificate. Four of these were amongst those who became paid sessional staff at the Southdown Project and continued for a number of years. As well as getting the training certificate, which he still possessed, one man recalled how I involved him in doing the illustrations for a short, practical book about youth work. He said,

> *It was great when Bob asked me to do the drawings for his book Resourceful Friends. He once said at a meeting that I drew the pictures which should be hung in the Tate Gallery. I've still got a copy of the book and the newspaper clippings about it.* (Nat)

The remaining three who took on long-term responsibilities did so elsewhere. Two still continue as leaders of church youth clubs. One ran a school football team and sometimes is paid to lead children's activities at a large holiday camp. He said:

> *When I worked there, the Southdown leaders came into my mind a few times. I remembered what they had to take and how they kept on smiling.* (Saul)

Four of the study group undertook full-time training and/or employment in youth work. Three of these will feature in the case examples in the next chapter. The fourth was a young woman who had been difficult at school and who fell foul of the law. She was given some responsibilities at the junior clubs and later took the Youth Training Certificate. She did so well that for five years she became a staff member at the Southdown Project. She not only organised the youth activities, she also developed in maturity and skills to the point where she was able to support and counsel other women. She recalled, 'I loved it. I loved working with Jane and Dave' (Thelma). On moving to another estate, she obtained a post at another youth centre which she stuck for three years before she had her own family.

It is gratifying for the former leaders of the Southdown Project to discover that 41 per cent of the former youngsters had themselves become involved in youth work. What explains it? Obviously, the Southdown Project provided opportunities. As they grew older, the young people were encouraged to get involved and to take on responsibilities. Perhaps, too, some saw the benefits of youth work and wanted to contribute in the same vein. One of those who just helped at the junior clubs now wants to change careers and take up youth work or a similar occupation. He said, 'The leaders gave me the confidence to be a leader. Now I want to be a youth worker or a careworker. I did apply to one centre but was told I needed paper qualifications. I intend to do this. I'll get less money but I've never worried about that. It's the challenge I want.' (Malcolm) The leaders' policy of giving some young people responsibilities within the project appeared to have three benefits. First, it provided much needed help at the busy clubs. Second, it often boosted the confidence and self-image of the participants. Third, it opened up the possibility that they could continue to contribute as they grew in adulthood.

Christian Influence

As explained earlier, the Southdown Project had a Christian element within it. It was administered by the Church of England Children's Society, ran a Christian boys' group called Jucos, and some of the leaders attended a chapel to which some of the youngsters also came.

Christianity was important to most of the leaders. They did not think it was something which could be separated into little boxes and just brought out on Sundays. They did believe it could be of help to young people. On the other hand, they did not think they had the right to impose their Christianity on youngsters. Dave, Jim and Bob were willing to discuss religion with anybody but felt that they should not initiate the subject. Interestingly, a number of the study sample had noticed this approach as the following comments show:

> *They didn't push it on you. We were all aware that it was there.* (Val)

> *We were aware that the leaders were Christians but you did not have to believe it if you did not want to.* (Tanya)

> *Jucos helped me understand Christianity. But I was never into it. I don't believe or disbelieve. You didn't have to take it on board if you didn't want to.* (Albert)

> *I admired Dave but he never tried to pump it into you.* (Ashley)

Did the Christianity of the leaders have any effect on the youngsters, an effect which lasted into adulthood? 28 said it did not, whilst 23 said it did. Of the minority who were influenced, 13 indicated that it definitely shaped their beliefs and practices, seven explained that it had a more nebulous effect on their general values, while three said that its importance was that it drew them into different friendship circles.

Of the 13 who considered that Christianity is a major factor shaping their lives, the case of Eric given in the next chapter is a good example. He was alerted to Christianity in his teens and reckons it is still a major force in his life. The effect on some others is seen in the following:

> *It (Christianity) made me see things in a different light. It changed my life. I had a friend who had cystic fibrosis. We'd known each other since we were very young. We became close mates, although we were very different. Because of his illness he couldn't do things I liked. He helped me in my Christian life. I was very upset and angry when he died. It put me down for a long, long time. I kept asking, 'Why?' I admired him. He kept on doing things he wanted until the last minute. He was at peace. Christianity makes me want to help others. I still believe. It's still there.* (Malcolm)

> *I used to go to Englishcombe chapel. It has stayed with me. Later I went to St Philip's church and we joined an Alpha group. We got married at St Philip's and I still see myself as a Christian.* (Rebecca)

> *I went to a Billy Graham meeting at Bristol and I went down to the front. For a while I kept it up and I went to meetings with Dave. Then I went back to the wrong mates and got into heavy drinking – whisky, lager, meths. While I was in prison, I went to the services. The chaplain got in touch with Dave and he came to visit me. Once out of prison, I left it again. I'd got married and one Sunday we decided to go to church – St Andrew's, and Dave and Jim were there taking the service. Christianity is still important. I don't go to church much but I cut the grass. My wife suffered from panic attacks and phobias about the dark. Nothing could help her. Then she went to a healing service and was completely cured.* (Wilf)

> *Jucos taught me to be patient, to understand people from different backgrounds. I was aware of God but my commitment to God came later. But what I do now has been inspired by watching the leaders and the way they worked.* (Archie)

The next quotations illustrate the views of the seven who regarded Christianity as having a less personal impact but a more general one on attitudes and values.

> *It showed us what is right and wrong. It was not pushed on us but it was a Christian influence. I like to go to church now but I don't go much.* (Ann)

> *The leaders were nice people and it influenced me the way they approached and spoke to other people. They never pushed it on anybody but we knew what they stood for. It made me more aware of religion.* (Dylan)

The main thing was that it made you respect other people. (Lex)

The three adults who pinpointed making new friends as the major impact were three who entered into the informal fellowship at the chapel. Sandy became a regular and commented, 'I went along to Englishcombe chapel with Bob on Sundays and there I became friends with John Davis who took it. I often went along to help him with the rags. I still believe but more so then.' The chapel was different from some of the youngsters' preconceptions about church as boring, orthodox, middle class and formal. It had services taken by working class residents of Southdown who displayed a Christianity which was serious yet fun. George had been brought up to go to church regularly and later rebelled against it. He found the chapel very different. He said:

> *There was a family atmosphere. John Davis and his wife were brilliant. I got friends. The same at Jucos. At camp I got to know one leader from Bristol, David Joyce. He too has gone through bad times – financially and mentally – and he has helped me. We've helped each other. I still see myself as a Christian. I'm not a classic example of a Christian. When it comes to the basics, I try to treat others as I want to be treated. I go to church when I can and I enjoy my friends who go there. They are more like me, the kind of bloke who finds it difficult to keep a car on the road.*

It can be concluded that a number, though certainly not a majority, of the study sample did find that the Christianity, to which they had been introduced directly or indirectly through the Southdown Project, had been and still was relevant to their lives, and had helped to shape their values and behaviour. This finding appears to contrast with that of Neil Bishop in his M.Sc. thesis *Can Christian Based Youth Clubs Reduce Delinquency?* He compared members of church based youth clubs with those of secular clubs and found that 'there was no significant difference between the behaviour of the two groups' (1998, p 42). Somewhat to his surprise, he found that the former did not major on presenting explicit Christian teaching in any of its programmes. Perhaps one of the differences in Southdown was that some of the boys were involved in a specifically Christian club, that several youngsters went to a local church, and that they often had everyday relationships with adults whom they knew to be Christians.

The leaders' emphasis on Christianity is not to imply that other faiths are irrelevant. Some of the values which informed the Southdown Project – such as a concern for the most disadvantaged youngsters – are found in other religions. What the project does show is that youth leaders can have a faith which influences the way they work and live without it being imposed on others.

Chapter Five

Their Stories

So far the study has considered themes and statistics which cover all the members of the study sample. Inevitably such an approach is fragmented and gives just parts of each individual. In this chapter, an attempt is made to present a more complete account of eight of the former youngsters. The accounts are made up mainly of what they said about themselves in the interviews. Essentially, it is their story.

Adam

Adam said of his home life:

My dad used to mess about with other women and he came and went. When I was 10 he made the final off. We were a one-parent family. My mother had three part-time jobs so I did not see a lot of her. I made her life hell when I did see her. I was out of control. Later another man moved in. We were always short of money. We had good times but I was often unhappy.

Adam was one of the first to call regularly at our house. Aged 13, he was a powerful figure who regarded himself as the new Elvis Presley with his greased hair, black jacket and jeans. Living close by, his mum called in frequently on her way to or from her cleaning jobs. She worked hard to provide for her three children but found Adam more a handful. She suspected him of glue-sniffing and stealing, she complained about his rudeness, and she worried about his schooling. And not without reason. Looking back, Adam said of his school days:

I got on alright but I had a big chip because I came from a one-parent family. I couldn't have the things which other kids had. I used to knock around with all the bullies. I got suspended for 12 days for hitting a teacher. He hit someone and I told him not to so he hit me, then I hit him. The classroom was wrecked by the rest of the class.

Spending much of his time on the streets, Adam welcomed the Southdown Project as a diversion and was one of the founder members of the senior youth club. He did not like football and cricket but was an enthusiastic darts and snooker player. He still remembers the clubs.

> *We went to Hallett's Studios. I remember having some fights outside. They were good times. The leaders could control it. Bob was serious when he had to be. He'd give somebody a stern look or tell them off but he wasn't bad tempered or snotty. We could speak easy with Dave. Jane was happy-go-lucky.*
>
> *We went on holidays. We went to Filey. Then Georgeham. I got sunstroke there and Jane rubbed cream on my back. Then I went to the Isle of Dogs with Bob's friend, Laurie. He taught me trampolining. I got silver and bronze awards for that. People laughed at me and said, 'What happened to the trampoline?'*
>
> *The clubs kept you occupied. You were actually doing something. Before we used to be on the street. My mum was working and when she was in she was ironing, washing, cooking, so she was glad if I went to the clubs. Everybody knew we had somewhere to go. We could all go and have a laugh and a chat. I always enjoyed it. You don't go back if you don't enjoy it.*

The attendance at the clubs did not diminish Adam's delinquency. As he admitted:

> *I was light-fingered. I started drinking at 14. I could get into pubs with older friends. I dabbled in soft drugs but not hard stuff.*

One day, Adam's mum called in to say that he had been charged with an unusual crime – ferret stealing. I discovered that ferrets were prized animals used to hunt rabbits. Adam and two other boys had nicked one from a neighbour. He relived the incident with laughter.

> *The ferret stank so we washed it. It climbed on the window sill and the neighbour saw it. The next minute the law was there. One of us tried to hide it down our trousers. We went to court.*

The leaders tried to get close to Adam. He often sat in the greenhouse and sometimes watched the TV with our kids. As our friendship grew, I felt able to challenge him on the street about his glue-sniffing, and persuaded him to hand over the glue which I poured down a drain. The indignant Adam then asked me to pay for it. Soon after, his mum called to complain that her watch was missing and that Adam had acquired a bike. At her request, I discussed it with Adam and initially he reacted angrily and stormed off. Later he returned and admitted he had swapped the watch for the bike. Together we visited the bike owner and retrieved the watch. Adam remembered these and other incidents in our relationship and said:

> *I often went to Bob's for help. I was very short tempered. I needed help. Once I nicked a padlock from a warehouse when I was out with Bob and*

Annette. I had no idea why I did it. They made me take it back. I had respect for them. Some kids knocked over their place. I would not do that. I only robbed people who wouldn't miss it. I went to court quite a few times and Bob spoke for me. I went about ten times and got put on probation and supervision and intermediate treatment. I went through a lot of rigmarole. I'm not sure if it makes you a better or worse person.

Given the serious nature of same of his offences – frequent shoplifting, breaking and entry, etc. – he was fortunate not to receive a custodial sentence. But, aged 15, the stealing did decline and, indeed, the court rescinded the orders it had imposed on him. At this time, Adam was one of the youngsters interested in Christianity. He said:

I was on the edge of becoming a Christian. A lot of people think that Christianity is going to church once a week, not smoking, not swearing. But there is a positive side. I've still got the bible that Dave gave to me.

Whatever the reason, Adam became much more co-operative and helpful. When one of his old partners in crime stole his dad's rent money, Adam refused to join him on a spending spree and persuaded him to come to me before too much had disappeared. Sitting in the street one day, he saw a friend cut his wrist with a piece of glass after being rejected by a girlfriend. Adam leapt to his feet to help and – always a bit clumsy – tripped over a brick. The wrist-cutter was alright but Adam was taken to hospital with a broken ankle. At least he could then legitimately have some time off school.

11.30 pm one evening he knocked on our window, following an argument with his mum. He had stormed out and declared he was not going back. We discussed his mum's nagging and I pointed out that much of it, like her current demands that he should be looking for a job, was an expression of her concern for him. I added that Annette and I sometimes nagged our children. Eventually, Dave Wiles took him home and made peace with his mum. Later we helped Adam in his job search. He recounted his work career.

I got a job with Bath Body Works. I stayed for two years doing panel beating. I then went into the building trade, one job after another. I worked with Dave Wiles' dad moving massive stones for his walls. One day we picked up old telegraph poles, I carried one in on my own and I remember the girls clapping me. Later I was a dustman for six years.

These young adult years were also marked by a return to crime. Adam explained:

I was into thieving from the age 18–22. Big stuff. We stole safes. On one job we had £22,000 between four of us. It was all from places we knew had insurance. I never got nicked but I got close. My car was seen and I was pulled in. The police told me I'd get a long time inside. It scared me. Now if my tax disc has three days to go I get jumpy.

Adam's determination to give up crime was also helped by his marriage at this time. But other problems were to arise as he told me.

I got married at the age of 22. The first five years were brilliant, although my wife had three miscarriages. After being a dustman, I went into railway engineering doing wheels and brakes for four years until I was made redundant. Then another engineering job. But then she started knocking about with her old girlfriends. She'd be out all day and come back out of her brains. The relationship crumbled. I asked her if she was seeing someone else. She convinced me I was paranoid. She got me to move out to give her some space. She was seeing someone else. I slapped her. Divorce procedures started. I was under a psychiatrist. This was due to drink. I was drinking 74 pints of rough cider a week. It gave me gout. I had angina and then a heart attack when I was 28. The gout and arthritis in all my joints has stopped me working. I have been registered disabled for four years and get Incapacity Benefit. I weigh 26 stone and take 18 tablets a day.

For all these troubles, Adam has found a measure of happiness with another partner. He said:

My partner is younger than me. We've been together six years, the best six years of my life. She works at the Dogs' Home. She is brilliant. We'd like to have children.

Adam appears to have stabilised although he can not work. He says that the Southdown Project was important to him and his friends and added, 'There would have been more doing a stretch otherwise.' But the credit for getting out of his adult criminality must mostly go to his partners and to his own decision not to risk a long prison sentence.

Colin

I met Colin before the project started. Watching an informal football match with my son, I admired the speed, skill and enthusiasm of a small, blonde-haired dynamo aged ten. We joined in and several times he slipped the ball and himself between my legs like a frisky wasp zooming between two broom handles. Later I met his mum who became one of my great friends. She was a middle-aged divorcee, bringing up five children by cleaning other people's houses and by being the church cleaner. She was both a regular churchgoer and a keen helper at the local Labour Party. Colin described his upbringing as follows:

I was brought up in Moorfields (a council estate near to Southdown) and we moved to Southdown when I was seven or eight with my mum, two sisters and two brothers. My parents were divorced but I didn't know the details. My dad lived in Germany where he remarried and I saw him once a year.

Money was always short. Even now when I get up and brush my teeth I am reminded of it because when I was young toothpaste was not always there. Same with washing-up liquid, they were not a priority, almost a luxury. It was hard. I only went on one school holiday to Yorkshire not to France. When you got those letters from school about holidays abroad, you knew you couldn't go.

It was such hard work for my mum. She had to work and do everything so we could not get a lot of attention at times. With that and my dad away, it is only in the last three or four years that I have come to terms with my feelings about it. For a long time it did my head in not to have a dad and you can't help but think what it would have been like if things had been different, if I had had more opportunities. But overall I had a happy childhood.

At school I was loud, quite noisy. Single parent families were not rare but were certainly in a minority and you were aware of it. I remember at dinners at school, families like ours were separated out. I was a great underachiever. I got five 'O' levels but I took 14. My reports always said, 'Could have done better'. I was disruptive now and again but overall I was not bad. Culverhay was quite a hard school and there were a lot worse than me. I got bullied a bit because I was small but not so much as if I hadn't been so loud.

I went to the Jucos and then to the Southdown Project. I have only good memories of it. It was great fun. I looked forward to it every week. Club in the evening, games on Saturday morning, meeting on Sunday. It is good to get together with lads your own age but it is also good to have a sort of protection. If you are in a group and they want to do something that you don't want to do, you can't get out of it. But that didn't happen when the leaders were there so it actually gives you more freedom.

Football was important to me, I was quite good at it. I didn't have the build or weight for rugby. Saturday mornings we used to walk down to the field, cold or wet, get changed on the grass and we were off. Later it was Southdown United. The project had footballs, cricket gear. To us they were like gold – a real football. It made a difference to us. I went to camp several times. I remember the bell shaped tents. We went to the beach at Cromer, played the wide game in the woods. I wouldn't have gone away otherwise. The leaders were a good cross-section. They complemented each other well.

Dave was almost like an older brother and could fight with and mess about with anybody. He was as fast if not faster, he could do anything and everything. But he wasn't boastful with it or rough. Bob did the organisation and kept an eye on us. It was good when Jane came, that added an extra dimension. I have no sad memories. I don't know if you filter out the bad ones but I don't think so.

I think of all the people I met I wouldn't have met otherwise. When you are young, the children you don't know are almost your enemies. But at the clubs all that was swept aside and you mixed with guys from other areas.

I was always at Bob's house. Most of the time I sat in the garden smoking cigarettes, playing swingball. My mate and I did a variation of that using a cricket bat. Sitting in the greenhouse as well. It was the focal point for our group. It was where we met every night, 'See you later, down at Bob's'.

From the start, Colin related closely with me. We made a rabbit hutch together. I took him all the way to Leeds to watch his favourite football team. Colin joined our family on our annual camping holiday. Colin had no problems with delinquency or truancy but he did need a relationship with an older male figure whom he could trust. He explained,

The relationship was something I was lacking. Bob was like a father figure and helped me in the sphere of confidence. Also I went to talk with Bob when I was going to college. It was difficult for mum to understand it so I went to Bob. He helped with the forms and the grant. Later I failed some of the exams in marine studies so I told Bob. Later I had some problems with my first serious girlfriend and we discussed that.

As indicated above, Colin went to college after school to study maritime studies but had to leave. He continued:

By this time unemployment was very high and I was on the dole for two years. I reverted into going to the project's building and I learnt to play pool. By this time, Dave was the leader and I began to help at the clubs. I was taken on as a worker, 30 hours a week which is classified as full-time. When Dave left, a local woman and I were running it. I enjoyed it. It was hard work, mentally it was arduous and I don't think I could have carried on much longer without professional training. I was there two years and during this time we went from being employed by the Children's Society to the local committee. I stayed far two years until 1988. It was a shame that Bob and Dave didn't carry on. The Children's Society seemed to change its policy. This stemmed from the report Faith in the City *which was about professionals withdrawing and leaving it to local people.*

I applied for a lot of jobs and then the MOD. (Ministry of Defence) took me on as an administrative assistant. Working in the Civil Service is incredibly male dominated and you have to know how to deal with people. You need confidence and my time with the project had helped me in that sphere. I have been at the MOD. ever since and am now doing an HNC in computers on day release. I love it.

I did have a few problems at the MOD. I had left college early and Avon Education Department wanted their money back and took me to court. I had to pay £5–10 a month back. I only finished that five years ago. I have been in debt but not serious debt. I had a large overdraft and one January I had no money in the bank and no money for the fare to work. I didn't have any food although I had paid the rent. I had to contact the welfare at work and they gave me an interim loan.

Soon after I started at the MOD. I formed a relationship and moved into a flat at Lansdown. Now my partner does the money and she works as well. It is not easy but I am in control and I'm saving a little each month which I have never done before. We have a lovely daughter. For my leisure I like to play pool, I play in a team. This year I am going to help with a caravan holiday for kids. A friend at work is the leader. My partner and daughter are going as well.

In the future, I want to get our ideal house, ideal for our daughter. Somewhere a bit quieter. I want to make my life as comfortable as I can. I'd love to move to North Devon, I went there five times with the project, such great memories. Walking along the beach in September when it is blowing. I want to give our girl the things I never had. Holidays and going abroad with the school.

If the project had never existed, I might have gone down an even rougher road and it would have been harder to lift myself up. You are open to influences when you are younger. In Southdown, if it is a winter night and you are out and there is just a group of lads and you are utterly and completely bored, you can end up doing anything to relieve it. My life would have been different. The project was one of my turning points, along with the MOD. and my partner. I would never have met the people who are now my friends.

Today we need Southdown Projects even more. Kids are changing and half of them don't seem to go out, they are watching TV cartoons and computer games. They don't seem to interact and socialise so much. They used to get together, to talk, to learn skills.

Eric

Eric's mum participated a lot in the activities of the Southdown Project. She came regularly to one of the mothers' groups organised by Jane Sellars, went on the outings to the seaside and always helped at the play schemes and fund-raising activities. Not surprisingly, her four children also became involved with the project. None more so than Eric who started attending from the age of nine. By this time his life had stabilised but previously it had been unsettled, as he explained:

My dad left just after I was born in Bristol. I'm not sure why. We moved to Weston. I was in a number of foster homes when my mum was ill and in some children's homes. You have to move in with a number of people you don't know and if you are five–six years old it is hard. There were no familiar faces – apart from my sister. It was totally different, you had to be in bed by a certain time. It was an unusual experience. So up to the age of eight there was no stability in my life.

After that my mum settled down with my stepfather in Southdown. I got on well with him. There were happy and unhappy times. My background has affected me, made it difficult sometimes to relate. I think it explains some of my moodiness and aggression and being isolated and withdrawn.

I spent most of my time playing football. I joined Jucos when I was nine. I really enjoyed club night, all the games, and I found the Sunday meeting more challenging and interesting than I expected. I went to the other project clubs and holidays and camps. I remember two of the Juco camps and going there in an old coach.

I felt the leaders were approachable and I could always talk with them. They did not condemn me. I got into the habit of going down to Bob's house because I knew it was safe, it was a safe environment. We always felt welcome. They never turned us away and even brought us cups of tea in the greenhouse or when we played swingball outside.

Culverhay secondary school was difficult for me. I tended to bully other kids. Few teachers took an interest in me. If they had done so I would have done better. The maths teacher did and I got a few CSEs.

Eric's mother became increasingly worried about him during his teens. She was concerned about his moods, his withdrawal and what she called his 'screwy' behaviour. She asked Bob and Dave to give Eric some individual attention. This suited Eric for he welcomed the opportunities to talk about his problems. He said:

At times I turned to Bob and Dave for advice. Like I could not always control my feelings. I know that my mum was worried when I went through a rebellious phase. Later I wanted to know more about Christianity. I think I became a

Christian when I was 12 but I did not keep it up because of the pressures of other youngsters. I became more serious about 15 and I began to help at Jucos. I also ran a small group, with Tim Tappenden, for young Christians. It was good experience.

On leaving school, Eric found difficulty in getting a job. He explained:

I went on a work scheme and did gardening with Age Concern for a year. I became an assistant supervisor. I enjoyed it. I liked being outdoors looking after gardens. It gave me pleasure to look after the gardens of the elderly. After that I was back on the dole for another six months. Then I got a part-time gardening job at Kingswood School which turned into a full-time one. It was looking after 30 acres and I stayed two years until I found it too repetitive and boring in the winter.

I left to go to Plymouth where I had friends. I was unemployed and got all the usual benefit cuts. I did a few in-hand jobs like carpet cleaning in hotels and cleaning a supermarket. Then another training course in clerical work including computer literacy which has benefited me now. I wanted to work with young people and moved back to Bath where I found a placement at Rackfield House which was for homeless people aged 16–64. I really enjoyed it. At the time I was homeless myself and was living in a church with a friend. After three months they put me on the work rota and I did sleep-ins. It gave me experience. A job came up as assistant warden and I got it. I was 24 and stayed six years. It was a stressful job because you were dealing with people with relationship breakdowns, alcohol, drugs, health problems.

Eric showed enormous persistence in obtaining jobs and then stuck at a stressful one for several years. His personal relationships were not as successful. A partner moved in with him. He recounted:

We were together for four and a half years. Christianity went out of the window. Then our relationship broke down. I think one reason people do go back to Christianity is that they lose someone very close to them. You have a hole in your life and it has to be filled. Whether it was right or wrong, I think the whole experience was beneficial to me.

It was not the only relationship breakdown that Eric faced. Later he was engaged, the wedding date was fixed and Dave Wiles was going to be best man. Then they decided not to continue. Eric said about the breakup:

I think Bob and Dave would have been proud of me. I stayed calm and objective throughout, which is a first. I must be getting maturer in my middle age.

Eric saw more of Dave Wiles during this time and did not allow the personal traumas to push him into depression. He got on with his life. He was determined to become a youth or community worker. He successfully completed an access course and then gained a place on a two-year Youth and Community Work Course at university. He did placements at local authority youth centres and successfully completed the first year. At the time of the interview, he was nearing the end of his final year and looking forward to a post in community youth development. While at college, Eric gave a lot of thought to Christianity. He said:

> *I attend church as often as I can and have found a church in Bristol which I like. Being at college has taught me about gender and sexuality which has caused me to question Christianity and the way it treats people. I try to see what the bible says about it and I find it very confusing because it is interpreted in different ways by different people. I have tried not to judge anybody but to allow God to do the judging. At the same time, I still find it a personal challenge.*

Over the years, Eric has always kept in touch with Dave and Bob. He had some considered thoughts about the Southdown Project.

> *If the project had not existed, I would not be where I am today. I'd be doing something like farming, going from job to job, living for today. I might have ended up in building. I would never have contemplated going back into education. Since I was 16, I've wanted to do youth work. I saw it in the way that Bob, Dave, Jane and Jim worked. I've got a lot of respect for them. It has taken me 15 years to get here but all my jobs have helped, office work skills, people skills. I think God has allowed it this way. It is like a jigsaw puzzle and the middle part has still to be put in.*
>
> *The Southdown Project was good in that it tried to understand and respect people's points of view and to find their positive aspects and to encourage them to work on that. If things did go wrong, they said 'Here's another challenge'. They didn't dictate to us or put us down. If somebody had something to say, they didn't think it silly, they listened. They gave advice at times but not in a way to direct people. That impressed me. The years 9–16 are important for development and we were encouraged.*
>
> *From the point of view of the 90s and looking back at the 60s, the Southdown Project could have been more issue based – sexuality, gender, racism, disability. They were not considered to be important aspects of youth work then. But this is with hindsight.*

Jack

Jack was from a Southdown family whose parents and four children had close links with the Southdown Project over ten years. Jack said of his own childhood:

> *Money was always tight. I got on a lot better with my mum than my dad. My dad had a decorating business at one stage but it all went wrong and that led to arguments with my mum. Dad was not a good influence on me. He really did not got involved with anybody. Bob went to court with him when he defrauded the gas board. He was expecting to go down but he didn't.*
>
> *But it wasn't a problem childhood. Mum's family were around in Whiteway. We three boys have all gone in totally different directions from dad. We would not even think of stealing anything.*

Jack was never any trouble in the neighbourhood and was unlikely to be drawn into delinquency. He tended to be withdrawn which may well have been linked with his partial deafness. His introverted nature and difficulties with hearing probably also contributed to his dislike of school. He explained:

> *I didn't like school and I stayed at home a lot. I had lots of operations on my ears and spent time in hospital. Usually my mum gave me a note to stay away although I did truant. In senior school, I only liked maths and geography but I was a long way behind.*

When he was about 11, one of Jack's friends, who also missed much schooling, took him along to the Jucos club. Jack took to it immediately.

> *There was the Sunday morning meeting and then the club night, first of all at Moorfield School. We had lots of fun fights there. Saturday we usually had football. It was real fun and caught your interest. It must have done because so many people went for such a long time. There was such a variety of things to do. I also went to camp and enjoyed it – even washing in cold water. We had spent our time playing football and cricket in our cul-de-sac and getting into trouble with neighbours. With the project we had somewhere to go. It kept me interested and I am a person who gets bored very easily. The big benefit, though, was meeting people. Before, you just met the same people. I never went anywhere with the school. It brought you out in the open and made you more ready for work. It brought me out of my shell and that has helped me now that I have to take meetings at work. At the same time, my mum went to the mothers' group with our little sister and that helped her.*
>
> *I also started going to Englishcombe chapel. I liked it because it was different to anything else I had done. Christianity came across as fun. I wouldn't say that what I did was best for other people but it was right for*

me at the time. I'm quite proud to say that I have never stolen anything or done anything really bad to other people.

We trusted Bob. I had found it difficult to trust people. He was the best man at my wedding. Over the last 15 years at work I have learnt that trust is the big thing. Later on Jane joined the team. She took some stick from the lads and took it well. We knew that if we had a problem, we could turn to the leaders and it would not go any further.

We used to go down to Bob's house at lunch-times and so I got used to going there. Then I went in the evenings to play swingball. My mum was worried about my schooling and had a chat with Bob's wife Annette. She agreed to see me a couple of nights a week. I felt embarrassed at first but it made me a lot better, so thanks Annette. Once I got into it, it was OK, it became second nature. The biggest problem in my life was reading and writing. I could have gone the other way, I could have blamed everybody else for my problems. Instead I went on to get two GCSEs.

It was thought that Jack might have difficulty in getting a job when he left school. Not so, as he explained:

I started stacking shelves at a supermarket. I worked my way up and am now the sales manager for one branch with a £3–4 million turnover per week and with 500 colleagues who work for me. I work unsociable hours and earn a high salary.

I see myself as a manager of people. For five years I had a similar position in a smaller store and in that time only two people left. I got on well with all the staff and some still ring me for advice. There are two types of manager, those who use their position to get something done and those who do it with people. I think I owe something to the Southdown Project because it did get me to meet more people and to become involved with them. Through the camps I met people from all over. At one stage, I thought I would like to do the same sort of job as the leaders but it was not to be.

Jack married and soon had two children. He was very successful at work but the demands of the job took its toll on his personal life as he tells.

I worked seven days a week. At one time, I did not get home for 13 weeks. We were moved to Derby soon after my wife had our first baby. She did not want to go and she did not know anybody there. She was depressed and had to see a psychiatrist. It was me. I got so much wrapped up in work. Later I moved out. The children are now 13 and 10 and are doing fine. I still pay the mortgage for the house which is near Southdown. My wife has grown a stronger person.

I live alone. I now take seriously stress at work. I know it can lead to heart attacks even amongst younger people. I know that my generation has to keep up with a younger generation in regard to computers. I now make myself go to the gym and I see a lot of my brothers. My personal life is not what I want it to be. I am happy in my job but I need to control it rather than it control me.

Looking back, I am glad about the project. It gave kids a bigger scope in life. Some of the lads would have been in worse situations than they are now. Some would definitely have gone down the wrong road. If we had not had the project, I don't know what would have happened.

Nicola

The interview with Nicola just flowed. It now follows without any comments and just as she spoke:

I lived most of my childhood in Southdown. My mum and dad were split up. My dad worked as a second-hand car dealer. He didn't have much to do with us. Occasionally we'd see him. When we were older, mum had a part-time job as a waitress.

I was definitely unhappy as a child. At the time you don't distinguish between being unhappy and happy. But I can remember looking at everybody else and really feeling inferior to them, even kids who didn't have anything special, who didn't have nice homes, nice cars. I felt inadequate compared with them.

From the age of seven or eight, I could distinguish between the haves and the have-nots. It was easier to play with kids with whom you might not have much in common except that you were scruffy kids. It was absolute poverty. I looked at other kids and they had more than I had, it was poverty that stood between us. I played with them as an infant, they were my friends. One girl in particular, we had been friends right through our childhood and we got to eight or nine and I went to her house for tea and I suddenly realised what a nice big house they had. Mum kept our house clean but it wasn't like her house. Then I realised that they spoke differently from us and her mum was very posh. It made me feel like shit. And that was the end of our friendship.

When mum went out to work part-time, it was easier. But even then money was always a problem. When I was five or six, I remember she did not have 10p for the electricity meter. Christmas you noticed it more – there were not the bikes. We were not running around the streets with holes in our shoes. Mum managed to feed and clothe us and that was it. We never went on holiday, didn't have a car, didn't get much for Christmas presents. There were not that many luxuries, no biscuits in the cupboard. The bare essentials, we just survived with no extras.

We all argued at home. It was the survival of the fittest. My brothers were always arguing and then mum would argue with them. It was like living in a war-zone. When dad was there – he did live with us off and on – there were major rows, really big ones between him and mum. Then he would be off and when he came and visited us there would be more rows because my mum would be really stressed. As the boys got older she couldn't handle them, couldn't discipline them, and she would let off steam against dad. She would say, 'He's done this, he's done that' and he would end up whacking her and she'd hit him around the head. I used to think that was normal. I didn't see anything wrong with it, I had to grow up tough, it was eat or be eaten. It was a very aggressive household. When my mum looks back at it I'm sure she thinks we were happy in Southdown and my brother and I look at each other in dismay.

I don't think I am being over critical but as I've got older and looked back I think my childhood is partly responsible for me not doing very much in life and not having any faith in myself. If only mum had said, 'Look, we may be poor but you are no different from anybody else, nobody is better than you because they've got money in the bank.' To me, being poor meant I was second class. I didn't understand that money didn't make you a good or bad person. I thought I was bad. If only somebody had explained to me that money is not what makes you a nice person. But I did not have that information.

I went to St John's school at first. When we moved to Southdown we could have gone to Southdown school but mum wanted us to have a Catholic upbringing. So every morning we had to go by bus to St John's and the bus fares drained mum financially. She had to take us to school on the bus and pick us up so she spent a fair chunk of her income on bus fares. I think if we had moved into Southdown school we would have mixed in easier. It took us a while to make friends then they all moved on to local secondary schools, Culverhay for the boys and Hayesfield for the girls, but we went to St Gregory's.

My two brothers were hardly at school. They were truants. I was the only one who stayed in. I used to go down to Bob's a couple of times but he made sure I went back to school. I never achieved anything. I came out with no qualifications. I was a bully. At that age when you are inferior you find someone who is even more inferior than you. The only way I could feel superior to anybody was physical strength because I came from a gobby household. I was a bit of a tough nut at school. I could not go up to make friends like you normally would. I didn't think I was a nice enough person to be able to make friends on your merits. I thought I had to pick on somebody. I remember, even when I was four, there were two friends and I had to muscle in and break it up. From birth I had been in this aggro family where nobody said you were a nice person. Even if you are pretty and intelligent you need to be told, you need to be told that you are special, that you are somebody. When we were 14–15 doing the mock 'O' level exams, I had no idea how important education was. Exams were for the posh ones. By the day the real exams came, I was down to eight CSEs and when they came I barely wrote my name on them and I didn't turn up for some. I wasn't in the duffers' stream. I didn't try very hard at school but I wasn't in the bottom lot. I wasn't as thick as I thought I was.

I suffered from eczema. When I was eight, my third brother came along and I took on a lot of responsibility for him. Mum had a part-time job, the boys were out playing and I would be baby-sitting. By the time he was three years and I was only 12 and going into puberty, I should have been out having fun but I also had him. I supposed it stopped me turning to crime. I had that responsibility and duty. It did me some good because, now I am on my own with a child, I've never thought, 'This is too much, I can't cope.' And I think I do it well. I've got to thank my mum for she gave me responsibility. At the time I felt sorry for myself.

I got involved with the Southdown Project when I was 10–12. I remember Bob and Dave and when Jane came on the scene. We were amazed that Jane passed her driving test. We saw the leaders as other authority figures but we knew deep down that they were not harsh. Bob used to say to me, 'You've got to go back to school' and I used to think 'You bastard' but I knew deep down that he was doing it because it was right. I remember having soup in his kitchen, hanging around his greenhouse and he was a really generous person. Who else would tolerate us hanging around the garden, smoking, playing swingball? Jane was nice to have because she was female. She used to take the girls to five-a-side football.

It gave me somewhere to go. We were hanging around on street corners. We didn't have anywhere to go. We used to hang around in the bogs at Roundhill. It would be raining and there'd be ten of us having a fag there. We used to go into the club when it was at St Barnabas' church hall. We used to look forward to it. They took us canoeing, ice-skating, things we would never have experienced. Ours was not the kind of area where your parents could say, 'we'll get the car out this weekend and go skating.' It was a deprived area. It's funny, the ones I looked up to, they came to the clubs and never went on holiday. The leaders took us on holidays and swimming at the Oasis in Swindon, that was like going to the Bahamas. We didn't do anything else apart from the project. Without the youth clubs, there was nothing.

As we got older, when we could have been going into town, some of us would have gone in for petty shoplifting. With a lack of money and nowhere to go, you can't just sit and read a book all day, you've got to do something physically and mentally. Things like canoeing were exciting, they were a challenge. Jane took us camping. We went on the Devon holiday. I was 15, coming up to 16, and that was the first time I had had a holiday. Up to then, I had been to the beach a couple of times and to Rode Bird Gardens, and that was it. Without that a lot more people would have gone off the rails.

The leaders took us places we would never have been able to go. More important, there was somebody there who understood why we were like we were. People thought we were riff-raff. They saw us as kids who were going to experience problems in school and home. They made a big difference because they knew what we were going through. We had somewhere to get us off the streets. We could have been burgling people purely because we were bored.

The project did have a Christian influence. The leaders were so fair to us. I used to think, 'Gosh, they're mugs' because we used to give them so much lip and abuse. We were going through those terrible teenage years. But they literally turned the other cheek. They reasoned with us. Our parents wouldn't do that, they didn't have the patience with us. That was the Christian in them coming out towards us. They could easily have walked away or been rude to us. They were never unfair to us, they never punished us with, 'Don't come down again'.

I left school at 16. Some of the girls went to college but I couldn't see the importance of education. I went on a Youth Training Scheme in the Owen and Owen department store in the bridal department. I didn't like shop work and after six months I took another YTS and went to a solicitors. I was really lucky, they sent me up to the university to learn touch typing but again I didn't see the importance of it. For the first time ever there was somebody giving me opportunity and I didn't take it. Then I worked for an accountant, then on to a telephone shop just when it became trendy to buy car phones. When the shop was closed I went upstairs to the billing office. That was closed. Then to a marketing department and they sent me to college as well and again I mucked it up.

They were good jobs for someone from my background. I used to look at myself and think, 'I'm a fraud. I shouldn't be here, I should be in a factory or working in Woollies because that's what my background dictates.' I used to worry to death that they would find out who I was—this person who grew up illegitimate in Southdown. This was when I started getting eczema because of stress. Even when they saw I had potential and paid for me to go to college, I didn't. Now I am having to pay for myself to go to college.

My mum moved to Norwich and it seemed a good way of escaping. Nobody knew me in Norwich and I felt it was a clean sheet of paper. But it didn't work.

I got there and my problems came with me. I wasn't into drugs, just occasional pot when I was 20. The years 16–20 should have been better. I didn't have to look after my young brother any more. But I wasn't prepared for relationships. I had my son Jonathan and had to find accommodation. Up to then I didn't have any dealings with the council. I split up with Jonathan's father and I was homeless. The council gave me a flat. It was the pits on this massive housing estate. It was full of mostly single parents, down and outs, druggies, violent families. They assumed that because you were a single parent you could be lumped in this estate. You were either one of them, out in the streets arguing with people and your kids were out with their nappies on playing in the mud, or you went the other way and locked yourself in, which I did, and kept yourself to yourself. But, as your kids grew up, they would play with others and end up like them. When my son started school, I went in a couple of mornings a week and helped out in the classroom. Otherwise I was very isolated.

As I was the only girl with three brothers, I had always been stuck with the baby-sitting, shopping and washing. I'd experienced my dad knocking my mum about and he wasn't loving towards us. In my young mind I assumed that men were not a loving figure to me. They were something I could do without. Yet I craved the affection of a man because I did not have it as a child. I didn't understand it during my teenage years. I've never been able to settle down. I've had relationships with rough, builder-type men because that's all I'm allowed to go out with because I'm not worth any more. I've got a lot of anger towards men because of being in a male household and because of my dad knocking my mum about. I couldn't understand why she had him back. Even now I wonder why she let him come into our lives. I don't do it with my son. But who am I to judge her? Relationships are a big NO NO. When Jonathan was six months, that was nearly eight years ago, I left Jonathan's dad. I've had two relationships since then. Both only lasted a year max. I've now been on my own for three years and will probably stay on my own for a good few more years.

In terms of my relationship with my son, I am very happy. My life revolves around Jonathan. He goes to bed at eight or nine o'clock at night. I go at ten. My life is my son. I see friends who've got children during the day, coffee mornings. Occasionally I go swimming. Within my personal life I am not happy. I can't work full-time so I am really unhappy there. I am unhappy with the way my life has turned out. I'd like to break out of the cycle of unhappy childhood, unhappy adult life, bad relationships. Some people go on and do the same as what happened in their childhood with their own children. I don't want this for my son. I didn't want children because of my unhappy childhood and Jonathan wasn't planned. I'm wary of having any more children because I don't want to end up like my mum with three or four kids all underachievers, police and social workers knocking on the door. She must have thought, 'Not one of you has ever amounted to anything'. But we now get on very well. She has always been there for us. She has never washed her hands of us.

I am hoping to go to college in September, just to do my English and maths. It's going to be a few years before I can work full-time and I want to get the qualifications I need for my own self-esteem, to get a good job but also to show I am worth something, to show that I am more than that seven to eight year old kid who ran around the streets of Southdown, terrorising the only two kids on the estate who I thought were worse off than me. I don't want to feel inadequate, to avoid people in town because I never achieved anything.

Every housing estate should have something like the Southdown Project so that children have options. When you don't have options as a child or young adult you are going to do what the group does, shoplifting, burglary, vandalism, joyriding. It is not going to work with everybody, some kids need more than the Southdown Project. We needed it.

Peter

Peter described his own background as average saying:

Dad was in one job and out of another. Once he was a bread delivery man and we lived on bread for about six months. Mum worked in a bar. Sometimes money was short but they managed to look after my sisters and me. The worst problems for them was when I started getting into trouble.

Peter was a strong, somewhat headstrong young teenager. He disliked secondary school.

I could not get on with teachers. I just could not be bothered. I was suspended twice, got threatened with expulsion, didn't take my exams. Later I got into fights. I beat a kid up and went to court. Then I went for nicking stuff.

When he was 13, Peter chummed up with a boy who was a regular at Bob's house. Peter explained:

I was in the street and Arnold said, 'Come to Bob's house' and we went and played in his garden. Then I started playing in the football team, I was right back. I went to the clubs – broomstick for a snooker cue, table tennis bats without any rubber on them. The music. I went to holidays at Georgeham. It kept me off the streets. Later I helped in the coffee bar and then with the games at the junior clubs – playing football and British bulldogs. I enjoyed it and it paved the way for my being a youth worker.

Peter initially kept his distance from the leaders but, in time, turned to them more and more. He approached them when he was in trouble at school and they accompanied him at his court appearances. He appreciated the help and said:

> *I'll never forget all that Bob and Dave did for me. They lived on the estate and everyone knew them. They were there. It's not like other clubs I've since come across where leaders just come in once a week and that's their lot.*

Peter's delinquencies declined and he continued.

> *At 15 I joined the navy. I didn't like the marching. I became a cook and got promoted twice and then demoted for fighting and drinking. I couldn't get on with officers.*

Despite these difficulties, Peter remained in the navy until he had a terrible accident. He recounted:

> *At 21, I had a serious motor bike accident and got flung through the windscreen of a car. It was only because of a passing ambulance that I survived, I was losing so much blood. I had multiple injuries, a paralysed left arm, broken ankle, my kneecap was removed, my left arm amputated. I was eight months in hospital then plastic surgery.*
>
> *After being discharged from the navy, I went back to Bath and retrained as a panel beater and paint sprayer. I worked in garages for a time then went back to being a chef. Then I was unemployed. I decided to leave Bath as the people I was hanging about with had beer and drugs as their main interest. I stuck a pin in the map of Britain and it landed on Hucknall in Notts.*

Peter followed the pin and explained:

> *I travelled to Hucknall, found a room then a flat. I was on Invalidity Benefit. I decided to do something. I took up archery as my main hobby. I use my teeth to pull back the string. I will be representing Great Britain at the European indoor archery games for the disabled.*
>
> *I went back to study. I got GCSE sociology, 'O' levels and an 'A' in social policy. I did a two year full-time National Diploma in Social Care. I wanted to be a youth worker and got a place on the Youth and Community Work course at a University. I dropped out after one year, I was sick of the political correctness, the other people on the course and the teaching methods. It seemed to me that I was on a conveyor belt and the tutors were churning out qualified, politically correct zombies that enter a youth club and haven't got a clue on how to interact with young people.*
>
> *I am a qualified part-time youth worker and I do sessions at the local youth centre. It's not the same as the Southdown Project. Most staff don't live in the area. You see the kids for about a minute at a disco.*

In Hucknall, Peter met his partner. He said,

> *We have been together six and a half years. We have a son, he is aged one and is teething and is a pain in the arse but a nice enough kid. My ambition is now to do a degree in catering and then manage a pub or hotel. I haven't got a temper now and I don't get into trouble. I would have got into more trouble but for the Southdown Project. It prepared me for youth work.*

Sally

Now aged 35, Sally was unlike most others in the study group in that she did not make her first contact with the Southdown Project through the youth clubs. She was a young mother who heard about and then came to a group for young parents held by Jane Sellars each week in Bob's house. Sally tells her story.

> *My mother left my father when I was seven in Bristol. I was sent to live with my grandparents. My mum moved to Bath and, when I was 11, I came to live with her and her partner. She did not know but he was abusing me for three years. Eventually my mum and I got a flat together in Twerton (close to Southdown). My two brothers had been living with my dad but were so frightened of him that they kept running away and they came to live with us. I had to give up my bedroom and sleep in the living room. Later we got a three bedroom house in Twerton.*
>
> *I was getting bullied at secondary school. In the fourth year, I wasn't actually expelled, I was asked to leave, I went to Cardinal Newman School. Because I was such a nervous type of person, I didn't tell anyone I was bullied but I was too frightened to go and I missed lessons. All I took was needlework. I really drifted along. I couldn't turn to my mum because she was in such a state. The closest people in my life were my grandparents and they gave me a little bit of stability.*
>
> *My mum was always in bed. I was the carer and I had to look after my brothers. If we wanted Sunday lunch, it had to be me or else we went without. She took an overdose and if I hadn't gone up to the bedroom she definitely would have died. There was no social worker, not even after my mum took the overdose. It was a very sad and difficult time. Inside I wanted to get out of that lifestyle. At 16, I got pregnant.*
>
> *When I got pregnant, my mum was very upset at first, it might have made her feel that she had failed. But once Melissa was born I was only there for six weeks and then I was rehoused. I didn't have a chance to grow up, having a child so young. I couldn't do what you usually do at that age.*

I used to visit a couple in Southdown and I heard about the Southdown Project and that you could be collected to go there an certain days and the children were looked after. I went along to the house and it became a habit. We did things in the kitchen and I can remember making flapjacks. We went places and there were interesting things to do. It was a really nice place to be. It was safe and had the feeling, 'We are caring about you.' It was great for the babies who were looked after in one room. It was a good feeling. I remember all the girls who went along. One was disabled and had a baby. She was later murdered by her ex-partner who killed her with a hammer. It was tragic. Jane was really helpful and friendly. The group was brilliant. It was like a base.

I always looked forward to being picked up, loading the carrycot on the minibus. Dave Wiles used to pick us up, he was a nice person. His Christianity was very clear. He was a very understanding person. But I can't remember him preaching at us. It was great because when you are at that age it is so young to have a baby. I think of my daughter who is now older than I was when I had her. It is too young to have that responsibility on your own. It is a struggle and if you haven't got anything to do or anybody to organise things for you then it must affect your own children. So I looked forward to being with everybody, with other mums of the same age and it was nice to think there were adults there who didn't just look at you and think, 'Oh, she's just 16 and with a baby, what kind of person is she?' I couldn't turn to my mum for advice. Possibly I'd have turned to Jane for she was very easy to talk to.

Eventually my boyfriend and I got a house and, when I was 19, we married. It seemed the right thing to do. Then I had my son when I was 20. I had met Bernie when I was 15. I came from a very unstable background and I think that subconsciously I just wanted to get out of it. But it did not work out. We separated when I was 23.

I had met somebody else. I didn't want to live with him so I went back to Bristol to live with my brother. I tried to keep Melissa at school in Bath because I did not want to upset her. So I used to travel from Bristol to Bath everyday. I also had a job in Bath looking after the elderly three evenings a week. So I used to take Melissa to school in the morning and pick her up at three to take her back to Bristol then back to Bath for 5pm. It made a lot of stress. Eventually I got this house in Bath. By this time I was divorced but my boyfriend started going wild. He was very cruel mentally and did a lot of damage over a six year period. I had Thomas by now and I didn't want the same things to happen to them as me. Eventually I got rid of him but he had demolished the house. It was six years of hell which brings us up to 1994.

Then Melissa who was 13 decided she wasn't going to school. I thought history is repeating itself even though I have tried hard to keep things stable and gave her things I didn't have, not just material things but love and attention, which made me feel worse because if I hadn't bothered I might not have felt so guilty. She refused point blank to go to school and I was threatened with going to court. She was not being bullied like me. She just didn't like it so I had to find her another school. On top of that I had her dad accusing me of not looking after her properly.

I am not married now. I have got a partner but we don't live together. Melissa has a job but Thomas now has problems and the teachers are concerned about his behaviour. I am finding that difficult to deal with. I have stuck with my children. It's taken a bit out of me and I've had stress-related difficulties. But I have really tried and done it in difficult circumstances. My own childhood was a really messy upbringing. I've given them a better childhood than I had. It proves that because you've had a bad childhood you don't necessarily give that to your children.

I used to hate going back to my mum's because she'd be in bed. I'd speak to her and she'd just grunt so I'd go out. It was no life. When I was 16, I used to go to friends' houses where the mum and dad were there and the dinner would be on the table and that gave a feeling of security. That's how I think you should do it. Now I am doing that for mine. I am still giving, making sure that my children are all right.

I am on Income Support now. I gave up work because I could not cope with the stress of that and Melissa. Also I found that when I worked I got Family Credit but I had to pay so much more rent and council tax that I was worse off. It disheartens you so much. It's a constant struggle. Buying something for myself to wear or something for the house never comes top of the list. I have to work out the money in great detail. You rely on buying things through catalogues. You pay more but if you don't do that you wouldn't have anything at all. I had a crisis loan from social security but had to pay that back at £5 a week. My life saver is a local shop where I worked for a while. It delivers the food on Friday but I don't have to pay until the Monday when I get my money. It is a skill to survive. But it causes so much stress. And now the government is cutting our benefit. There is not much more they can take away. I hardly ever get out and I've been quite depressed. I've got a friend along the road who is in a similar position so we can relate with each other.

I'd like to be with somebody in a good relationship, the kind of life where people are nice to each other and talk to each other. I want security, I feel quite insecure and I'm sure it goes back to when I was small. I'd love to be involved in voluntary work. I see myself doing it because I sympathise so much with children whose basic needs are not being met.

I remember when I was finding it hard, asking the social services if there was somebody who had been through my kinds of problems who would come and talk with me. But there was nothing. I needed the Southdown Project again because there everybody was in the same boat, their children were the same ages. When people in the same situation get together it makes such a difference because you just support each other. I think the Southdown Project had an effect on me and I didn't really realise it. It wasn't a passing phase. It gave me a little bit of security and direction. It was something to look forward to. If it hadn't been there I would not have met all the people in the same position as myself. Nobody judged you. You didn't have to feel ashamed. When I heard that Bob was moving, I was really sad.

Wynn

Wynn was one of the earliest youngsters to be close to the Southdown Project. At that time his home life was not happy. Looking back, he said:

Mum and dad didn't work so resources were very limited. I got on well with my mum. My dad almost lived his own life separately, I never saw much of him. He enjoyed his drink most nights. The worst times were when he came back and picked on my mum who'd get kicked. It was a sad childhood really. But whatever happened, mum made sure that we ate properly. It must have been terrible for her. I did a paper round and stuck up skittles just to get some cash.

At the age of 13, Wynn spent much of his time outside of the home and soon met me in the street. He became a regular caller at our home where his quick-witted and ready tongue endeared him to my Glaswegian wife, whom he nicknamed Mrs Haggis. He attended the planning meetings to set up the youth club and, after it started, never missed a club. He remembered:

I went along with the rest to Hallett's Studios where we had to hump everything in and out. Next we held it in Ascension Church. I ran the cafe. It occupied me. We did a lot. There was football every Saturday until I broke my foot. I remember the project's first van, a little Fiat. We were at Batheaston Youth Club when Bob came and picked us up in it for the first time. As soon as big Adam sat on a seat, it broke.

The first holiday was at Filey. Then we camped in the grounds of a college in Plymouth and there were weekends at Georgeham. I stayed with Bob's friend Laurie on the Isle of Dogs – I still think of it when I watch the marathon on TV. I did trampolining with him and got a certificate. He had an Austin van and we used to go to the college and get our hair cut for nothing by the students. We used to visit his mum. We spent a New Year there.

During these years, Wynn was not doing well at school. He explained:

I got on terrible at school. Very rebellious. Whenever anybody tried to tell me, I knew better. At 13, I was really kicked out of school. Most of the rest of the

time I spent with the project. I now tell kids to go to school, it is so important.
I can see now that I was a total fool – you were not big you were stupid.

The project leaders formed a close relationship with Wynn's teachers. The leaders attempted to get him to attend school. The teachers kept us informed of how he was doing. On one occasion, they found him so uncontrollable that they phoned Dave and myself and we collected him from the school and occupied him at the project for a couple of days.

Outside of school, Wynn's waywardness soon brought him to the attention of the police. He was fined for house-breaking. Other misdeeds followed. He said:

> *I went along with the group. I went shoplifting. I got dared to pinch a scarf*
> *from Woollies, got caught and taken to court. I went for driving a motor*
> *bike under age.*

The project leaders were concerned about Wynn's unhappiness at home, his flare-ups and other problems at school and his delinquency. With his and his parents' agreement, they agreed on a three-fold strategy. First, to give him more responsibilities. The aim was to improve his confidence and sense of self-worth. Second, to encourage him to identify even more closely with the Southdown Project so that he had something of which he could be proud. Third, to be available to him both when he wanted to talk and also when he was near to emotional explosion and wanted to calm down.

Within the senior club, Wynn was entrusted with going to town to buy its new records. He was soon acting the part of DJ, a skill which later led him to running discos. Within the junior clubs, he was expected to help the leaders keep order and to entertain some of the members. The outcome was that he was soon spending three to four evenings a week at the clubs. As he put it:

> *I had no money to do anything else. It was boredom all down the line. We*
> *had three boys in one bedroom. We never had stereos or electronic games*
> *or computers. The only holidays I ever went on were at the project. Being*
> *in all the activities became a learning curve because I always had a bit of*
> *get-up-and-go in me. It gave me opportunities. When we did Jucos at*
> *Moorfields School, Bob and Dave used to drive the lads home and I used*
> *to put the kit away. I never shied from work and you learnt from it.*

It was not just the clubs. Wynn came every day to the house. He said:

> *I remember the house as if it was yesterday. There was that big Chesterfield*
> *settee where I was always fighting Bob's son, David – friendly fights. Perhaps*
> *it was good for David because he saw a lot of different lives and he could realise*
> *that what he had in Bob's family was different from lots of other families.*
> *Sometimes I wanted to chat about things at home. I often felt down about home.*

The strategy seemed to work. Wynn took his tasks at the clubs very seriously and acted in a responsible manner. He even had a talk with one junior member and advised him not to steal. He accompanied me when I gave talks about the project and, in the after-talk refreshments, he would convey his enthusiasm for and pride in the Southdown Project. He almost became a part of our family, often staying to meals. When alone we talked about Wynn's inability to communicate with his dad, his conflict with his eldest brother, his tendency to flare-up. His delinquent acts were frankly discussed and means of avoiding them set out. I always accompanied Wynn to court and spoke on his behalf to the magistrates. On one occasion, he was placed on a supervision order with a requirement to undergo Intermediate Treatment. However, the magistrates recommended to the probation officer that this be served with the Southdown Project.

Wynn did stabilise. But his last year at school saw problems there. He was accused of stealing or receiving school dinner tickets which were then resold to pupils. He often truanted and was threatened with appearing before an educational attendance tribunal. A concerned teacher came up with the idea that Wynn be attached to the project for three days a week on the school's work experience scheme on condition that he attended on the remaining days. It clicked. Wynn enjoyed being treated as a staff member of the project. The leaders showed their trust by allowing him to bank monies. He took a leading role at weekend camps, especially in erecting the tents, he organised the lunch-time soup club in which some youngsters came in for a soup and roll at the house before being driven back to school. One educational crisis did occur which he later wrote about as follows:

> I went to the technical college to do a catering course. We had a woman teacher and she was moany. When she told me to take my coat off, I refused...she said 'If you don't take it off I will have to make you go back to school.'
>
> As I started weighing out the flour, I said to the boy next to me, as a joke, that I would beat him up. As I said it, there was a teacher in front of me. He said. 'Stop looking at me like that' and that he would kick me out so I said I would save him the energy and left. I went up to Bob's house to sort it out.

We did sort it out after Wynn apologised and he went back to school and settled down to write about the project as part of his CSE course in English. It also involved an oral in which, the teacher confided, he was never lost for words.

Next Wynn appeared at court on the dinner ticket scam. Again I spoke on his behalf and said how well he was doing on the work experience scheme. We were worried, given previous warnings, that he would be sent to approved school. The magistrates listened and then fined him heavily. Wynn had difficulty in paying the weekly contributions to the fine and was summoned back to court and warned of the consequences of not paying. The project leaders then worked with Wynn to ensure both that he could pay and also that he was taken down each week to do so.

So Wynn left school without losing his liberty. Now he could go out to work. He had never shunned hard work and, in his case, it was to be 'salvation by works'. He immediately applied for a job as the boy on the greengrocer's van. He said:

> *I was over the moon when I got it. I ran all the way back from Twerton and straight into Bob's and said 'I've got the job. £40 a week.' I had to get up at 4 o'clock in the morning. It was tremendous hard work, 9–10 hours a day. I loaded all the stuff at the fruit and veg market.*
>
> *Then I went to the Careers' Office and I got a job at a big shop. I have now been here 18 years and I'm the area manager over 21 shops with a £10 million turnover. I've done it through hard work and determination to succeed. I've done a course in computers because we are going over to that.*

Outside of work, matters did not run quite so smoothly. He explained:

> *I was 16 when I jumped in the deep end with my first girl and we married at 19 although we didn't have kids until I was 26. I'm an outgoing person, she is not. I was working long hours, had to go in early, I was on call-out. We divorced. The two girls are with her and she has remarried. The older girl phones me when she wants to come over. I remarried as well. We have no kids. My wife is brilliant, very outgoing.*
>
> *I know money isn't everything but you can't do a lot without it. You can't have a nice home, car, furniture. Whatever happens, I've got a nice pension and insurances. I've got a good wage and money in the bank. I'm committed to the firm. I work six days a week and come in at 6.15 in the morning as I like to clear my desk before people start ringing. There is a possibility of becoming a director.*

So Wynn seems to have made it. His second marriage is stable. He has a highly paid, demanding and satisfying job. He is disciplined enough to keep himself fit by running regularly and doing workouts in the gym. Given his poverty-stricken background, his unhappy relationship with his dad, his problems at school and his early delinquencies, his present position is remarkable. Most of the credit must go to Wynn's personal qualities, his persistence, drive and ambition. In addition, he acknowledges that the Southdown Project played a part. He said:

> *Without the project I would almost certainly have got into more trouble. If I had been kicked out of school permanently what would have happened? What would have happened if I'd been sent away?*

Chapter Six

The Essence of the Project

Was the Southdown Project successful? It depends on what is meant by success and how it is measured. A small project with limited funds could do little to improve the incomes, housing conditions and job opportunities of residents. Outsiders now often judge success by government benchmarks which demand statistical evidence that delinquency has lessened or that the number of children taken into care or custody has declined. The original book *Kids at the Door* was able to publish figures, collated by a co-operative official of the local authority Social Services Department, which demonstrated that in the first three years of the project the number of offences committed and the number of children removed from their homes on the estate did decline. But it was not possible to collect figures for this small area in succeeding years. Moreover, such figures about children would not be wholly appropriate because this study was also interested in what happened to them as adults.

The thrust of the study, therefore, was to ask users to make the judgements, to ask them what they thought about the project and its influence. Such an approach does produce numbers and they are recorded in previous pages. But they are not objective numbers measured by academic experts from outside. They are subjective numbers which emerge from the opinions of participants. I am comfortable with this approach for I believe that, in the end, what counts is what local residents and users consider to be significant.

Most of the former users who were interviewed were enthusiastic about the project. This may partly be the result of the kind of former youngsters who were tracked down and did agree to be interviewed, although my assessment is that there was not a great difference between them and those who were not interviewed. It must also be said that there were some young people (and families) with whom the project did not engage and a few with whom it did not cope and with whom contact was never maintained. Amongst the 51 who were seen, criticisms were not completely absent. Some of the women pointed out that initially the leaders provided insufficient activities for them. One of the men, who was by then on a youth training course, criticised the project for not dealing fully with issues of racism, sexuality, gender and disability. The most frequent criticism was that I left it too soon. As Lex put it, 'The worst thing Bob ever did was to leave. He should have stayed.' Adam added, 'I was disappointed what happened to the project after the first leaders left'.

Drawing upon information supplied by the study sample, it was possible to construct a means of measuring their vulnerability to certain disadvantages and of the way they did turn out. The vulnerability ratings suggested that 39% were at 'high risk', 31% at 'moderate risk' and 29% at 'low risk'. Yet in their late teenage years, only two were judged as displaying 'very unsatisfactory behaviour', 22% were giving some 'cause for concern' while 76% were 'satisfactory'. Only one of the youngsters was taken into public care and none received a custodial sentence. In adulthood, 2% were considered to be living 'very unsatisfactory lives', 12% as 'unsatisfactory' and as many as 86% as 'satisfactory'. Just seven of the study group had been in severe criminal trouble: in short, many of the youngsters turned out far better than might have been expected. It is not being claimed that the Southdown Project was the only or even the main factor in the youngsters' lives. Their development was shaped by their parents and extended families, by their peers, schools, jobs, partners and a multitude of other influences. Rutter, Giller and Hagell point out that some young people prove resilient in the face of 'severely negative experiences.' (1999, p 206). The reasons are not known although they suggest that the resilient youngsters are characterised by high intelligence. Certainly, the study found it was those who had inner qualities which made them change direction. Thus Syd, who had been heavily into drug abuse and dealing, said that he enjoyed the Southdown clubs but, at that time, he had no desire to change his habits. It was later, aged 19, when a close friend was sent to jail, that he decided, 'it was time to call it a day'. Others seemed to mature once they settled with partners and children. Dylan said. 'I gave up drugs once I met my partner and I gave up smoking once we had a baby.' None the less, a large number of those interviewed did claim that the Southdown Project both made their childhood more enjoyable on a council estate and also positively influenced their personal development despite the disadvantages surrounding them. Interestingly, a number finished the interview with words like 'If it was not for the project, I don't know what would have happened to me'.

So given that the Southdown Project had some successes and was seen as valuable, the question is raised, what made for its positive effects, in short what was the essence of the project? The answers to this question are drawn not just from the interviews with the former youngsters but also from interviews with eight parents who were closely associated with the project and with Ray Jones who was an early volunteer and later became Director of the Wiltshire Social Services Department. They also spring from conversations with former staff of the project and from my own involvement.

I will argue that the usefulness of the project came from the following:

- Its three main services, namely the clubs, the greenhouse base and the individual relationships.

- Four primary factors which made the services both more effective and long lasting, that is the fact that the leaders lived locally, that they displayed certain leadership features, that the project won considerable community support and that it was long-lasting.

- Three contributory or secondary factors which consisted of a strategy which pursued a mixed not a specialist approach, positive co-operation with other agencies and the availability of jobs for young people.

Ordinary Youth Clubs

The clubs run by the Southdown Project were certainly ordinary and probably somewhat old fashioned even in the 1970s – ping pong, snooker, darts, an old record player in inadequate, rented halls. Yet they attracted youngsters and, when asked, all the study sample spoke enthusiastically about the clubs, the trips and the holidays. They were asked what benefit these activities were to them and Table 10 presents their answers. In this case, they could give more than one answer so the columns in the table will not add up to 51 and 100%.

Table 10. – Benefits Received from the Youth Clubs

	No.	%
Countered boredom	29	57
Prevented trouble	21	41
Friendships	18	35
Personal growth	13	25
Satisfied parents	10	20

Thus 29 of the former youngsters stipulated that the clubs countered boredom. 21 said that the activities prevented them getting into trouble by providing an alternative to crime, vandalism, drug abuse and glue-sniffing. The two categories are linked, for studies do show a link between boredom and juvenile offending, (West and Farringdon, 1977). Some examples of what the study group said are as follows:

It was something to do in the evenings. Most of us went. We didn't have to hang about the streets and cause trouble by running around. It kept the boredom away. We'd have got ourselves into a lot of serious problems. It was rough and the clubs quietened it down. (Sandy)

It was a case of going to the clubs rather than hanging about the streets. If it wasn't for the clubs, who knows what I'd have done beyond smashing windows. What can you do without money? (Matthew)

It kept us off the streets. I'd have got in with the wrong crowd and been in trouble. There are people who did not use the clubs who are now a lot worse off than I am. I had a hard childhood and it gave me enjoyment. I used to race along after school to get on the snooker table. (Saul)

I was very aggressive. I'd have probably have got involved with gangs. I used to get out a lot of my aggression playing British bulldogs, football, wrestling on the mats. (Malcolm)

We had nothing to do, we didn't have money. Otherwise we'd have hung around with the wrong crowd. (Ann)

I would have been hanging about the streets and might have got into glue-sniffing – like some did. (Bella)

It gave kids something to do. There would have been a lot more trouble. The drugs problem would have been a lot worse. (Jill)

We didn't have to hang around. When I look back, most of my happy memories are with the project. (Rebecca)

It was always somewhere to go, people to talk to. I really looked forward to the holidays because I didn't go away. Otherwise we would have got into a lot of trouble. (Joy)

We had so much fun. I'll always remember the holidays. If it had not been for them we would probably have got into a lot of trouble because we were bored with nowhere to go. (Mal)

The clubs stopped me getting into the wrong crowd and into trouble. (John)

It kept me off the streets. I would have done a lot worse than I did. We'd have got into more trouble because there was nothing to do. At the age of 15, if I said to people that by the age of 34 I still would not have done a day in prison, they would not have believed it. It kept us out of trouble that we could have slipped into ever so easily. All our family has kept out, which is remarkable considering how many years dad did inside. (Tyson)

Syd perceptively pointed out that the influence of the clubs was not entirely for the good because he met up there with some of his pals who used drugs. But he added, 'If I hadn't gone to the clubs, I don't know where I'd have gone'. After the interviews were completed, a reunion was held at which about 40 attended. It divided into three groups to reflect upon the past and group leaders recorded the main findings. One major view was that the Southdown Project had provided youth amenities which had not been there before, which the local authority and other voluntary agencies had not installed. If it did nothing else, the Southdown Project ensured that a group of youngsters had safe and enjoyable leisure, and that was important to them. But it did do more than that, for, as the reunion group also recorded, it took some of them through 'troubled times' and held them back from crime and court appearances.

18 of the study sample considered that the clubs helped them by finding friends and by making them feel part of a group. This is not to say that they did not make friends elsewhere. Rather it was that the clubs both gave them a safe environment in which to meet with their friends and also the scope to make new ones. Given that social isolation and loneliness are factors associated with anti-social behaviour, then the friendship aspect may have played a part in keeping some out of trouble. The interviewees made comments like the following:

I still see the friends I made. We were all there together. It definitely had an effect on me. It became a focus of our lives. (Nat)

Friendships. I got a lot out of it because it was vibrant. I made new friends. I remained friends with one boy although he was a couple of years behind me. (Archie)

The friendships were great, kids don't mix so well today. At the camps we all got on well together with kids from different parts. (John)

It showed me the value of a family. I don't mean my own family, I mean the family within that group of people. To this day I still talk to every single one of them – even the ones I used to fight. (Matthew)

The clubs made you belong. Everybody was there and you enjoyed the atmosphere. It was a family atmosphere. (Malcolm)

I got depressed. I used to go to the project. I can talk to people now. (Wilf)

At the time it was a godsend. Somewhere to go and meet people. I don't know what I'd have done without it. (Roland)

It was a get together, we did things together, had a chat, went to places together. (Lex)

13 of the former youngsters said that their involvement in the clubs helped their personal development. Two commented that at the clubs they experienced and began to appreciate a sense of community. Sometimes the leaders put on role plays about dealing with everyday situations and Mal may have been referring to these when he said, 'I learnt to stick up for my rights. Later when the council would not put gas in this house, I took them to court and won.' Some mentioned that they learnt new skills in how to discuss and relate with each other. But the word most often used was 'respect', Nat said, 'It taught me to have respect for others. It changed me'. In like manner, Lex commented, 'It made me respect people. It made me grateful for what I've got. So I have kept out of trouble'. At the Southdown re-union, one of the groups used similar words when it reported that the clubs 'taught us to respect others.' The mixing with others, especially on the holidays, seemed to instil a greater respect for other people, a respect for their rights and their differences.

Ten of the study sample added that one of the benefits of the clubs was that it reassured parents about what the children were doing. Sandy said, 'My parents were always worried about what I was doing and if I was getting into trouble. If they knew I was at the clubs, they were happy'. Tanya observed, 'My parents were glad to know where we were, who we were with. My mum wanted to know what we were doing. But if we said we were going to the clubs or to Bob's that was OK'. John commented, 'My mum couldn't have afforded to take us away so she was happy for me to go with the club'. As Donald put it, 'It was safe'.

The clubs served to lessen boredom and provided an acceptable alternative to anti-social behaviour on the streets, they were a base for friendships which gave company and emotional satisfactions and, probably in a small way, they enabled some members to develop personal skills, particularly those which facilitated getting on with other youngsters. These benefits occurred with the approval of parents and saved some from the parental questioning, which they found so annoying, about whether they had been getting into mischief.

More Than a Youth Club–the Greenhouse

Yes, the youth clubs were an integral part of the Southdown Project. But not the only part. Also important was the greenhouse, that unpainted, ill-repaired, draughty, lean-to against the side of the house. It had not been foreseen as a part of the project but gradually became a meeting place for about a dozen teenagers, until they were replaced by the next generation. During the winter they huddled together inside, avoiding the spaces where the rain dripped through, and in good weather sprawled out on the paving slabs, known as 'the patio', to play cards and then, more energetically, swingball.

The importance of the greenhouse was that it was their place. The leaders did not intervene save to bring in some coffee and to be on hand if required. As teenagers, they needed to have some private space, to be on their own apart from adults, apart from the authority figures who seemed to run their lives. As Ann put it, 'It was like our club. We used to knock on Bob's door and then go in the greenhouse. l don't know how they put up with us. They gave us coffee.' Nat spoke in similar tones, 'We played on the patio, swingball, two-a-side football, it used to get quite heated. Bob's son David was a dab hand at swingball. Then in the evening we dashed to get the best armchair. We just talked. There was no glue-sniffing. It was brilliant, it was our meeting place and when I walk past the house, I still think about it'.

As with the clubs, the greenhouse was acceptable to parents. Jill observed, 'We used to play cards in the greenhouse. We always knew that somebody would be down at Bob's .We all got on well together. Some came down at lunch-time for a soup. My mother was strict on what time we had to be in and she knew we were in safe hands with the leaders because she knew them.' Tyson explained that they liked being in a place 'where there weren't many rules, we rebelled against that' and that their parents liked them being in a place where they knew their children were safe.

The greenhouse was different from the youth clubs. It was less organised, smaller, restricted to a certain number. It gave them space for their own group activity. It gave the youngsters the satisfactions of their own company within a safe and legitimate environment. Simultaneously, it brought them into closer relationships with the leaders who opened the door and dropped in with the coffee.

Individual Relationships

The Southdown Project was more than youth clubs. It was also more than a greenhouse. Central to its existence was that it also facilitated individual relationships. But these features can not be completely separated. It was at the clubs, the house, the greenhouse, that youngsters got to know the staff and feel confident enough to approach them. The study sample was asked, 'During your teens, apart from your parents, to whom would you have turned if in trouble?' 43 replied that they would have approached the project staff, some adding that they would have done so even before their parents. For instance, Matthew said, 'I couldn't talk to my parents about my troubles. I did some silly things when I was in the wrong crowd'. In like manner, Jill said, 'It was easier to talk to Jane than my parents'. Of the eight who would not have turned to the project staff, five said they would not turn to anybody, two would have gone to friends and one to another relative.

The question was a hypothetical one and does not signal that they actually did seek out the staff. In fact, as indicated earlier, 33 of the youngsters did talk individually with the leaders about a personal difficulty or need. The matters they discussed were often multiple and interconnected. For instance, a youngster who came to discuss his shoplifting might also talk about his truancy and a bust-up with his parents. Table 11 indicates the main single difficulty the individual brought to a leader.

Table 11. – Main Subjects Discussed with a Leader

Delinquency	10
Parental relationships	10
School/college matters	3
Pregnancy	3
Care of their own babies	3
Employment	3
Problem with peers	1
Total	33

The individual relationships can be split between short-term and long-term. Some of the short-term relationships concerned immediate crises. Tyson recalled, 'I had some trouble with my dad. He got angry and threatened me. I ran to Bob's house as a safe place. We had a talk and he took me back.' Jill turned to Jane and explained, 'I got pregnant when I was 16 and Jane helped me through that and helped mum sort it out. I had an abortion which Jane helped me to organise. She took me down and brought me back.' Joy approached Jane in similar circumstances. She said, 'At 16, I got pregnant and went to see Jane. I had a difficult decision about whether to keep the baby or not. I decided I had to.' Mal stated, 'When my parents split up, I ran away. I went to town and wandered around. I didn't know what was happening. The leaders helped me through.' Other short-term relationships were not immediate crises but were important to the youngsters. Thus Wilf sometimes dropped in to see Dave. He said, 'I turned to Dave when I felt down. I was worried about having to go to court.' Matthew remembered, 'I didn't know what to do when I left school. I'd done work experience. I went to talk it over with Bob.' In the case studies in the previous chapter, Nicola is an example of a girl who called in when she wanted something explained. Jack came regularly to the house for a few months while Annette tutored him. Peter turned to the leaders when he wanted them to accompany him to court.

Relationships with a core of other youngsters were long-term, perhaps involving daily or weekly contact spread over years. Agnes was a young mother who suffered violence from the father of her child. She said, 'Jane stood by me and got me out of a mess. She would sometimes give me money when I didn't have any. I used to get soup at Bob's. Jane came to court with me.' Wynn, from the previous chapter, was constantly in Bob's company. He came round five times on one Christmas Day and, in *Kids at the Door*, his ins and outs were shown over a seven day period' (1981, pp 50–51). Adam and Colin also maintained close contact over several years, the former frequently seeking help to stop his nicking, the latter coming for adult friendship. Arnold was another who was always around. He explained:

> *My dad was never in. He'd go to work at 6, be home at 6, then go out so I hardly saw him at all. It was important that I could go down to Bob's, better than staying at home. Bob used to come to drag me out of bed and get me to school. It made me do a lot more than I would have done. My mum turned up at school one afternoon when Bob was taking me back. He took her back to his house for a talk. Then she wrote to me threatening to commit suicide if I didn't go to her. I went down to see Bob. I thought she would do it. Bob came to court with me a lot, I got done for cars, for vandalism, for poaching. I got a suspended sentence once. I couldn't have stood being boxed up. The project kept me out of prison definitely. It got me a job.*

Saul recorded:

> *I got depressed because of all the arguments at home and I needed someone to talk to. I went down to Bob's house. Our house was a mess and I didn't like staying in it. My step-dad was such a slouch. I couldn't live like it.*

Occasionally, the relationship was strong enough to allow youngsters to stay with a leader during a time of crisis. Anthea always looked up to Dave and she remembered, 'Before I went into care, I stayed with Dave and Donna'. Others came when the position at home seemed at breaking point.

Usually, a youngster chose to associate most closely with just one of the leaders. Thelma sought out three of them at various times. She said:

> *My mum asked Bob to have a talk with me about not doing what I was told, being cheeky and skiving off school. Then he and Dave came to school when I was in trouble for setting the fire alarm off. Later, when I was in court on a charge, Bob came and gave me a character reference. Then, when I was living with a bloke, I used to go to Jane with our personal problems. I could go to Jane with anything.*

These lengthy relationships seemed to go through definite stages in the following manner.

- Initially, the children attended the junior clubs during which time they got to know the staff.

- If they required more help, they usually moved into a closer relationship at the ages of 12–13 years during which they enjoyed dropping into the house and going out in small groups.

- The most intensive contact happened at the ages of 14–15 when their personal and social difficulties loomed large at home, school and community. This was often the period when the leaders were actively attempting to restrain the youngsters' behaviour, to control their tempers, to stop them fighting, to desist from truancy, to give up stealing. The result could often be tensions between leaders and individual youngsters with the latter perhaps storming out, verbally abusing the leaders and even physically threatening them. The relationships were at their most intense.

- On leaving school, the contacts tailed off but were maintained with the staff making it clear that they were still available. At this stage, the young people tended to see them as some kind of elder statespersons whom they could consult and, in some cases, take on as a role model. The exceptions were the young women who had children and then the contacts might be maintained at the same rate. In some instances, the individual relationships continued for the full decade. Indeed, some have kept up contact with staff until the present.

It was in these individual relationships that the leaders came closest to and probably had the most influence with the young people. What was the nature of these relationships? They were not statutory officers. Within statutory contacts, officials often possess weighty powers, which can be used as a means of control, and extensive resources, such as financial grants, training facilities and residential placements, which can be used to promote their interests. The staff in the Southdown Project had no legal powers, the relationships between them and the youngsters were voluntary, and they had few material resources. Another difference was that the project staff saw the individuals within their own neighbourhood, not in offices, and saw them not just in interviews but also in clubs, on holidays and on the streets.

So the relationships were not akin to official ones. Yet they were not the same as everyday friendships in which persons, usually in the same age group, are drawn together by mutual liking and keep each other's company because it offers them emotional satisfactions. The project leaders and the youngsters did seem to like each other. The relationships might contain aspects of everyday friendships in that they might have a game of cards, watch the telly together, bicker over which music to play. But they were between people of different age groups and the relationships were based on an agency in which records were kept. To describe the relationships offered by the leaders, I use the term 'resourceful friendship.' The leaders were employees of an agency who brought certain values, skills, resources and purposes to the relationships. The values included respect for the youngsters and a belief that they were as important as the richest child at public school. The skills, as I have elaborated elsewhere, included the capacity to engage with individual people, to counsel and advise them (Holman, 1983). The resources included both the facilities of the South-down Project and the personalities of the staff themselves. The purposes were varied. Of course, at times the relationships were like ordinary friendships in which the participants joked, laughed, ate together and gained emotional pleasure from each other. But these pleasures were a by-product of a definite purpose which covered enabling a child to go to school, reducing loneliness, preventing delinquency, obtaining a job and so on.

The resourceful friendships appeared to be wanted and appreciated by individual youngsters for two main reasons. First, they gave time. Wynn said of the friendships, 'It was a one-to-one. At school there were 38–40 kids in a machine. There was no quality time whatsoever. The teachers were under pressure. The leaders listened to us when there was a problem, they sat down and chatted with us.' Over-burdened parents sometimes could not give time. The leaders, generally, were available, they were interested, and they had time. As one of the groups at the reunion wrote down, 'The project was a drop-in. You could get help when you needed it.' Second, they gave advice and support but not in an authoritarian manner. True, within the project settings, the staff had to keep discipline and exercise some control. But they did not possess the rights and authority of teachers, social workers and parents. They did not issue orders or threats. It was this participative, warm, mutual kind of relationship that the youngsters seemed to want. Perhaps Malcolm put it best, 'There was something missing in my life that what Bob and Dave gave was able to fill. They were for us'. Ray Jones observed, 'The leaders were very significant people to the young people. They became role models'.

Youth clubs often provide positive leisure and peer friendships and certainly these happened at Southdown. However, unlike most youth clubs the Southdown ones were allied with the opportunities to form resourceful friendships with the leaders. These opportunities arose, as will be mentioned shortly, because the youth club leaders also lived in the area and were available to callers. To be sure, the friendship had dangers and pressures. One danger was that individual youngsters might become too dependent upon the leaders, another that it might create a barrier between them and their parents. The pressures were that the leaders often had enormous emotional and time-consuming demands made upon them. But the leaders were agreed that the individual relationships were the core of the project while the interviews showed that the former youngsters regarded them as a major means of improving their lives. Matthew concluded, 'They brought out the best in us. They encouraged us, made us come out of ourselves. They were for us, always willing to help. They gave me the confidence to be a leader'.

The services of clubs, the greenhouse and individual relationships did not exist in a vacuum. They were built upon and enhanced by four main factors.

Leaders Lived There

The first was that three of the four main full-time project staff, lived in Southdown while the fourth was nearby. Such residence is in contrast with statutory social workers and other professional staff who tend to commute in and out of the deprived areas where they work and who are not around in the evenings, at weekends and Bank Holidays. As Matthew put it, 'It was not run by people from outside. The Southdown Project was local people. Outsiders may be from a better upbringing but they are not the community.' Tyson explained, 'The leaders were not simply people coming in and then going off with nothing really happening. They were there 24 hours a day.' Nat commented, 'Bob lived there and the house on the corner became a landmark.'

Being resident, the leaders soon became known to the locals. They met in the same shop, chatted on the same buses, Bob's children went to the same schools. These constant contacts meant that local people could evaluate the leaders. They also meant that the leaders could assess the needs of the area and identify those who might eventually get involved with the project.

Not least, living on the job made the leaders available. As Wynn put it, 'Anybody could knock on the door at any time – and did. When was there not somebody in the house being helped out?' Ray Jones said, 'I can remember being at Bob's house some evenings and kids would come round, perhaps chucked out of home, having to be in court next day, in trouble for not being at school. There was availability, accessibility and acceptability.' This availability reinforced the growing perception of the youngsters that the Southdown Project was a part of their lives. They did not have to wait days for an appointment and then travel into town to see an official. Of course, most of the kids at the door called for comparatively trivial matters about the time of the next swimming trip, to borrow a bat, to pay a deposit for the holiday. But they could call at almost any time and every contact served to build up relationships. And, at times, it was important that a staff member was available straight away. The youngster who had stormed out of home, the teenage girl who thought she was pregnant, the tearaway being pursued by a violent gang, the worried boy who had just been questioned by the police, the young worker who had just been sacked, they wanted to see a trusted adult who could help them at once. There is little doubt that the availability of the staff, the fact that they were there, impressed the youngsters. As Jill put it, 'They lived there and so were part of the community. If anyone had a problem, they could go down and sort it out.'

Availability had its drawbacks. Meals were interrupted. Bob's children sometimes got fed up with answering the door. Once Dave Wiles started courting Donna, he wanted some privacy! But, overall, living in the area was a positive feature of the project and one that convinced the youngsters that the leaders were doing more than a job.

Leadership Style

Living in the locality would have been of limited use if the attitudes of the leaders were off-putting to youngsters. The second main factor was the leadership style of the staff. The study sample was asked about the leaders. In answering, they mainly referred to Dave, Jane, and Bob. Mentions were also made of Jim Davis who joined later and Tim Tappenden and Cathy Bright who served shorter periods especially when Dave was away on a full-time social work course.

Nearly all those interviewed spoke positively about the leaders. This bias may be hardly surprising given that the study sample was drawn from a number selected because of their association with the project over a number of years. Those who disliked the staff might soon have withdrawn from any contact with the Southdown Project. None the less, the opinions of the former youngsters on the style of the leaders do reveal the attributes which they considered both important and useful. Most informants gave multiple answers but the following table identifies just the main factors to which they gave prominence.

Table 12. – Main Factors Identified About the Leaders

	No	%
Friendly	18	35
Approachable	10	20
Trusted	9	18
Lived locally	8	16
Good organisers	6	12
Total	51	100

Figures can not fully express what the study sample said. Here are some examples for each category except for living locally which has just been discussed.

Friendly

> *They were very friendly. We didn't see them as authority. They told us off if necessary. The community was involved. The leaders were there. We could go round. All the youngsters fancied Jane – we'd say. 'Can I do anything for you Jane?' There was always something for us to look forward to.* (Albert)

They were relaxed. They needed a lot of patience. They were good, friendly people. (Seb)

They were alright because they were not bossy. We could have what we wanted within reason. And Jane–we could rib her all day and it didn't affect her. (Arnold)

Jane was lovely. More like a friend. (Ann)

They never seemed old before their time. They came down to our level. They let you have fun. Very easy to talk to. (Joanna)

Approachable

They were approachable – even Bob, and he had them in the house all the time. You could talk to them. (Val)

The leaders listened. They were not strict. They were like our mates. Jane was wonderful. Game for a laugh. But a terrible driver. (Nat)

Jane was great. I don't think of her as much older than us. We could relate to her and talk about clothes. Dave was good fun. We could talk to Bob about anything. They had a hard time looking after us and took a lot of stick from some of the boys. I don't think I could do it. The leaders were all very down-to-earth and everyone got on so well with them. (Jill)

We felt a part of it. I got on really well with Dave. It was like one big family. It was a one-off. It made a lot of difference that the leaders lived there. I don't think you'd ever get people like that again. There were lots of things to do. It gave us a sense of belonging. (Thelma)

Trusted

The leaders could be trusted and the parents also trusted them. (John)

Dave was our sort of person because he'd been in trouble with the law. But he changed and we looked up to him and everybody got on well with him. He was a sort of idol really. Bob used to get on well with everybody. He organised holidays and football. They were down-to-earth sort of people. (Ashley)

Good Organisers

They gave us different things to do every week. They were not strict like school. They kept control but that was it. (Mal)

They were willing to do all the activities. They were there. (Lex)

The leaders made it. They were fun and lively but also there was good organisation of games, they always had ideas for things for you to do. (Thorpe)

They were organised but not too disciplined. They were not lax – it wasn't anarchy in which anything goes. (Dylan)

According to the former youngsters, the leaders had a friendly, relaxed approach combined with the skills of organising activities. The outcome was that the former attended the youth clubs on a regular basis. The leaders were also both approachable and to be trusted so that the youngsters were ready to approach them for individual help. The leaders were resourceful friends. It might be asked where did their style come from? None had been trained as youth or community workers. Bob had a qualification in social work, Jane a social science degree and, later on, Dave and Jim went on social work courses. The answer is a combination of personality, in-service training and experience. By character, none of the leaders were authoritarian and they tended to be tolerant, friendly and blessed with a sense of humour. They all possessed certain attributes which could be exploited in youth work, Jane loved to chat about pop music, fashion and boys; Dave was athletic and musical; Jim was great at romping around with the younger kids, swimming and laughing with his contemporaries; and Bob could talk endlessly about football teams, tell corny jokes and beat all the kids at table tennis. Their in-service training entailed going on occasional courses but also meant the weekly team meetings and hours spent talking with coffee cup in hand, at which approaches and strategies were hammered out, how best to deal with disruptive kids, should the ribbing of Jane be allowed to continue, how to draw in more withdrawn youngsters. With regard to experience, Bob had been involved in youth work for much of his life and tended to know what kind of activities and games went down well. Jane and Jim were still young enough to recall their experiences as club members. And Dave had the experience of being brought up on the estate.

Of all the team members, Dave was probably the crucial one. Many of the youngsters had known him before the project started. He was one of them. The older ones had known and even feared him as the Southdown tough nut. Adam recalled, 'I can remember Dave as a skin head. He used to walk up the road in wide trousers which were about three inches below his knee and old Doc Martins and a Prince of Wales crombie. You didn't say much to him in case you got a kicking. We feared him. Then he changed and we began to speak to him.' Dave changed through his Christian conversion and the awe changed to respect and liking. As Adam continued, 'Dave was someone to look up to. He understood because he had been there himself. He came from the same background as me.' The youngsters appreciated that Dave had been through many hardships similar to their own. He was a neighbour. As Dan put it, 'Dave Wiles lived opposite me. He was so easy to get on with.'

In the beginning of the project, Dave's friendship with Bob was significant. The young people seemed to reason that if Dave thought the project was alright and was entering into it then they would do the same. They could communicate with Dave because of his enthusiasm for heavy metal and rock music – which always remained a mystery to tone deaf Bob. As time went on, some found it easier to speak with him just because he had encountered, and overcome, similar problems to their own. Certainly there were young men who could relate with Dave but not with other team members. They observed Dave keenly and Nat noted, 'Dave only just kept his temper once. One boy sprayed him with a hosepipe and I saw the look in Dave's eye, for a second I thought he was going to lose his patience but Dave held out.' Remembering Dave's background and his former lack of self control, youngsters perceived that change was possible. But Dave did not rely just upon his background. He started to study, developed youth work, social work and then managerial skills. He married and settled down with a family yet still remained in the area.

In the early years of the Southdown Project, Ray Jones made a study of Dave. He said in an interview with Bob that 'Dave became a major resource for the community and carried a lot of credibility with young people'. However, he also pointed out that:

> *Initially it was difficult for Dave. He had been in bother himself. Now he was being employed to work with young people and had to take on a new image, almost a new identity. He had to work out new relationships with some of the people on the estate. He achieved it very quickly. Another difficulty for him was working out whether he was in a real job or not. His dad seemed to think a real job was working with your hands. The next issue became how he could limit the demands made on him. He had to pace himself so that he was not burnt out.*

Ray wrote up his study and part was published in an article called *Living and Working on the Patch* (1983). In it he concluded, 'Dave had shown that the "new careerist", without any formal training, can make a major contribution to the provision of social work services'. The staff of the Southdown Project all displayed styles which facilitated the work. But particular mention must be made of Dave Wiles who pioneered a little known approach, that of the locally born and bred full-time staff member.

One of the skills which Dave later developed was that of training others. As some of the teenagers began to help at the play schemes and junior clubs, so Dave perceived their potential. With the help of Ray Jones, he designed a training programme which was spread over six months and culminated with a residential course. The trainees had tutorials to discuss how they were doing in the clubs and, in groups, identified what made for good and bad youth leadership. Those who successfully completed the course were awarded the Southdown Youth Certificate. They were an expression of the community supporting the project.

Community Support

Community support was the third primary factor which bolstered the services of the Southdown Project. The definition of community has provided academics with many publications. Bell and Newby collected 94 definitions and concluded that they fell into two main categories. There were those which saw community as a readiness to identify with a common place or territory and those which perceived it as the sharing of a common interest, (1971). Southdown could certainly be seen as a community in the first sense as it contained residents, many of long-standing, who regarded themselves as Southdowners and were concerned about its well-being. Community used to refer mainly to small locations. In recent years, it has embraced larger territories as in the term the European Economic Community. I therefore now prefer the term neighbourhood which Jeremy Seabrook defines as 'an area where the majority of people know by sight most of those who live there and probably recognise everyone of their own age group (and) know all the significant buildings', (cited by Henderson (Ed.), 1995, p 14). The essence of neighbourhood is that geographically it is small whilst relationships are numerous. However, I noticed that in Southdown most people spoke about community so I will use the terms interchangeably.

Neighbourhoods should not be over-romanticised. There was no golden age when neighbours never quarrelled, when gangs did not fight, when theft was non-existent, when every person joined in street parties. None the less, the support or hostility of a community can be crucial to the success or failure of local organisations which, in turn, may either help or hinder the neighbourhood. In Southdown, it was clear to the leaders from the start that increased youth activities, which often involved noisy youngsters waiting outside the project house or building, could annoy some people. Moreover, I knew from previous experience that residents could expect youth leaders to exert control over 'wild kids' in the streets even outside of official youth activities. I knew too that, as the level of youth events increased, so some families were likely to complain that their kids were being left out. Grumbles, resentments and complaints from adults can drive a wedge between youth work and the neighbourhood and so slow its progress.

Reasons like these contributed to the Southdown Project being set up as a community project not just a youth one. It was acknowledged that children and young people were best helped within a framework not just of their peers but also of their families and community. Simultaneously, the involvement of adults, especially parents, should not be so overwhelming as to drive away teenagers who were at a stage of life when they wanted some independence from their families. The needs of youngsters, adults and the community had to be held in balance. Thus, from the beginning, staff visited all local homes to explain the nature of the project and to seek the views of adults. As one of the groups at the reunion recorded, 'after us, the grown-ups got involved. There were trips for everyone.' The trips were mainly coach outings to the seaside and theme parks which were open to all residents. Family trips were organised to go swimming. And on Bank Holidays, it became a tradition to hold games on the field in which dads played the boys at football and the mums took on the girls at rounders in often very heated contests.

The appointment of Jane Sellars marked a significant step forward. She formed two groups for parents which met in the house. Jane soon devised a varied programme of crafts, talks from health visitors, visits from hairdressers plus jaunts to outside leisure activities. One of the groups was mainly made up of very young mothers and contained a crèche in one room for the babies. The other group consisted mainly of mothers with toddlers. Adults were thus drawn into the project.

To be sure, the drawing in of adults did lead to some voicing disagreements over what the project should do and where the outings should go and, occasionally, by some flare-ups between members. Some residents obviously felt that too much was being done for families who should be doing more for themselves. But overall the strategy worked in the following ways:

- Many local people did begin to view the project in a positive light. The frequent conversations between them and the leaders, often in the course of an outing, enabled information to be spread and policies explained. One particular topic often raised by the adults was why the leaders were so tolerant towards the badly behaved kids and did not sling them out of the clubs. The leaders then had the chance to explain their methods. Certainly, criticisms about the project appeared to be reduced.

- Once the role of the project was understood, a few neighbours began to express concerns directly to staff. Examples were of a child being left alone in the evenings, about suspicions of drug abuse, about youngsters seen vandalising property.

- In a modest way, the Southdown Project was fostering community spirit. One of the parents, Martha Hatt, observed, 'It wasn't like other youth clubs because it did things for parents. So it got the community together.' After one outing, I recall a parent saying, 'This is the first time we've done something together'. Parents were not only acting together but also adults and youngsters were participating together. The local support gained for the project contributed to its work with the young people.

As adults became more involved, so more began to help at the youth activities, particularly with the junior clubs. Parents, in particular got involved. Brian Bateman was a somewhat elderly parent whose own boys had grown too old for the clubs. He became a regular helper who specialised in playing draughts and other board games with the juniors. Cynthia Pool told how, 'I got on ever so well with Jane. Then there were play schemes in the holidays so l used to help and take my daughter along'. Significantly, some became helpers after they had been helped. Toni Millbank had been to a professional counsellor for her personal problems and was told about the mothers' group at the project. She recalled:

It was so brilliant because I hadn't been meeting anyone. It changed my whole life. It brought me out of myself. I began to help out at the summer play schemes and I could take the boys to them. Later I ran the play schemes. It taught me how to do arts and crafts and to run children's groups.

Catherine Hull had been moved to Southdown after a painful marriage breakup and she and her three children found it difficult to fit in. She remembered:

It started when Bob knocked on the door to welcome me to Southdown. Jane was lovely, she was welcoming and so non-judgmental, a person I admired a lot. Dave too. The leaders were all good friends and we had some good laughs. Then Bob helped me get away for a break when I got depressed.

Catherine then accepted an invitation to help at the clubs where she used her considerable artistic talents.

Martha Hatt had moved to Southdown with her husband and four children from a previous marriage. She joined one of the mothers' groups in which she found friendship, fun and a close relationship with Jane. She then became a helper at the junior clubs and accompanied Jane on camping trips with the girls. Jacky Field was a divorcee who brought up five children on a very low income. She appreciated the fact that the project welcomed adults. She never went on holidays yet accompanied the project on holidays at Filey and Georgeham. She too became a helper. Initially Jacky insisted that her only contribution was to clean up. Gradually she became involved with the children and eventually took on much of the responsibility for running the before-school club.

As more and more parents joined in so they became appreciative of what the project was doing for their and other children. To quote Toni Millbank again:

Thorpe was a bit of a handful and volatile at times. By him going to the clubs and mixing with other children and doing sport, he seemed to be able to control his temper. He loved the camp. If the project had not been there, crime would have been much higher.

Catherine Hull spoke in similar vein:

The project was a saving grace for us. It made life bearable at a time when we wanted to get out. It was like a bit of light in a dark time. Phil is not a group person but he was able to trust Bob who was a bit of a father figure. It was very helpful to my children. The project created a space for kids and kept them occupied. The kids there were so wild that without the project it would have been hopeless.

Molly Toner was another mother who became a volunteer after attending the mothers' group. She said, 'My kids enjoyed the clubs so much, they were always there. Kids used to get into a lot of trouble but they got better after the project came.' Cynthia Pool added, 'It was good for children. It kept them off the streets and gave them a purpose.' Another supportive parent, Martha Ifford contributed, 'I never had to worry what the children were doing. I would look around and they were gone and I used to think, "It doesn't matter, they are down at Bob's". It wasn't a problem.' Martha Hatt commented:

I always had problems with Eric because he was a very inward child. He was destructive. He was deaf but this was not found out until he went to school. The only way he could express himself was by breaking things. When he joined the youth clubs and the church, he started to come out a bit more. He was always down at Bob's house. He became totally different. He has got on so well and is a real credit. I am very grateful to the clubs for what they did for him. Now I am going to college to see him get his certificate. If it hadn't been for the clubs, a lot of the kids would have gone astray.

Jacky Field said:

We didn't get holidays so Colin really loved the camps. He was very sensitive and quiet. He needed pushing out. He needed a man and related so well with Bob and Dave. He became a helper and later became a leader. He couldn't have done that without the project.

Brian Bateman summed up:

It became a habit for children to go to the clubs where it was free and easy. The project became the centre of attraction. Quite a few would have got into drugs and I can think of a boy near me who the team definitely kept out of trouble.

The involved parents did not have to rely upon second-hand information. They saw what the project was doing. As nearly all became enthusiastic, they contributed towards local backing for the project which was one of the main factors why, unlike other short-term efforts, it continued to help children for over a decade.

Further, as more local people participated, so they saw the limitations of a project based on a house combined with erratic use of church halls. Suggestions were made that the project needed its own building and they took an active part in fund-raising so that, as explained in the introduction, after a few years the Southdown Project obtained its own new premises on Roundhill. Once in the building, the clubs and activities expanded rapidly. Much more help was required and this, again, came from local residents with some acting as volunteers and others being paid as sessional staff. Dave Wiles was responsible for much of the recruitment, support to and training of these local helpers and he has reflected upon their contribution. He identified four major gains from their involvement.

- Local helpers, much more than outsiders, understood neighbourhood issues and dynamics. They knew what current pressures the club members were undergoing in their homes and schools. Such knowledge enabled them to work with more understanding of the children concerned. Further, Dave stated that they were 'accessible when difficulties arose, they were seen as more helpful, approachable and trustworthy than those social workers based in offices some distance from the estate'. (Jones, 1983)

- Locals were usually already known to the club members who, therefore, were the more ready to turn to them at the clubs, whether it was to stop them being pushed off the pool table, to prevent them from being bullied, to partner them in a game, or for some reassurance and comfort.

- An empathy often existed between the local helpers and youngsters because they had often been through the same experiences in terms of material hardship, of feeling devalued at school, and, in some cases, of being delinquent.

- Not least, the helpers often gained something themselves in that they grew in confidence as they did well at the clubs and received the regard of children and other parents. Dave explained, 'people with problems tend to think that's all they are. The project tried to help them see they had strengths. They were able to help others and they re-formed their view of themselves'. (Interview made by Dave Wiles for an Open University tape, 1990.)

- Ray Jones added a fifth benefit, namely that it broke down any divide between staff and others. He said, 'Sometimes I would turn up and it was difficult to say who was the volunteer or sessional worker and who was the person who had come along with some difficulty. There was no status divide. Sometimes the sessional workers could have personal crises so they could be either side of the fence. Barriers were broken down'.

But Dave was not blind to some of the disadvantages of local help.

- He pointed out that they had to face some role conflict 'in that one moment they were a member (of the neighbourhood) and the next a leader who has to exercise authority. Their friends might find it difficult to see them in this new role'. (Wiles, 1990)

- The helpers also faced some of the pressures of the full-time staff. They had to regularly attend the clubs even when feeling worn-out and there cope with scores of demanding children. Some also experienced kids knocking at their doors with questions about the clubs' activities.

- They did not always receive praise from neighbours. Dave reported an example where 'unsupported suspicions by some local people that money contributed by residents was being misused by those who offered to organise events and accusations that the helpers' children were gaining more benefits from the clubs than other children', (Jones, 1983). Such remarks could be voiced on the streets. Further, differences could occur between helpers as to how clubs were being run and jealousies could surface between volunteers (who were not paid) and sessional workers (who were).

Despite these disadvantages, Dave and the team were in no doubt about the value of local help. The expansion of activities within the new building could not have occurred without them. Their involvement then had other implications. The local helpers began to form ideas and proposals of their own which they fed to the leaders. In time they were invited to team meetings and they contributed both to the minutiae of planning each club programme and to policy discussions. It was at this stage that a breakfast club was started, that the cafe was kept open longer hours with a more varied menu, that a room was let out to a self-running club for elderly people and for a judo club. A users group was established to oversee developments in the building. Almost without realising it, residents were being trained to take over.

This book concentrates on the first decade of the Southdown Project when Dave Wiles, Jane Sellars and myself were the main leaders and when the Children's Society underwrote the expenses – howbeit often with grants raised by the staff. For the sake of continuity, and as already indicated in the introduction, it must be added that by the end of this period the Children's Society was keen to withdraw the extent of its support, that I had moved to Glasgow to initiate another project, and that Dave Wiles was eventually to be given a wider managerial brief by the Children's Society within the West Country. A Community Association was formed to run the project, to raise money, to appoint staff. Who were its members? They were mainly drawn from the local helpers. Brian Bateman, for instance, became the treasurer. Dave recalls 'a woman with difficult children, who was taking valium, whose husband was a compulsive gambler: she became a volunteer and developed as a motherly figure to whom others could turn to for advice.' (Wiles, 1990) She too was elected to the Community Association. Who were the staff? Again, they were recruited from those already involved. Toni Millbank became a capable leader – yes, the same Toni who first came to the group with her own problems. Catherine Hull, by the way, moved on to organise student community action at a college.

The Community Association always found difficulties in raising money. I am now on the committee of a locally controlled project in Easterhouse, Glasgow, and I know that such independent projects can succeed only if they have access to proper and regular grants from outside for obviously they are in deprived areas which lack money. None the less, the Community Association did enable the project to survive for another decade. It can be concluded that the policy of rooting the Southdown Project in local community support not only improved its running in the first stage but also fostered the continuance of its benefits to another generation of children in its second era.

Long-term

As just indicated, the Southdown Project endured. This long-termism is the fourth vital factor behind the usefulness of its services. Users of statutory social services sometimes complain that social workers soon move on. They dislike seeing two or three different officials about the same matter. My observation is that the staff in voluntary projects do stay longer but that there is a tendency for the projects themselves to be much more short lived. Family centres, community projects, youth initiatives, etc., tend to receive three year funding at best. Sometimes national voluntary societies regard their local projects as innovative, demonstration projects which they run-down after an initial impact. At other times, they close them in order to fit in with the latest fashion for which central government is offering money. Short-term ventures may suit staff whose main concern is their own career advancement and who can use the experience as a stepping stone to the top. But they do not suit local users. Once projects start, local expectations are raised as to the future, and disappointment and disillusionment can follow if they close down after a limited period. When I first moved into Southdown, I was visited by the three Labour councillors who obviously considered that after 12 months I would be returning to the academic ivory tower.

The essence of the Southdown Project was not just that the staff lived there but that they stayed for 11 years – and some residents considered that too short. Dave and Jim continued in the area for even longer. From the start, the team wanted to endure even though the funding situation was often precarious. Looking back now that the initial youngsters are all adults, the benefits are even more obvious.

Long-termism is essential if the needs and strengths of an area are to be fully understood. Just getting to know the geography of the estate, knocking on every door, identifying local institutions, meeting teachers, staff, social workers and police took months. Becoming part of the community included, for some of the team, worshipping at a local church, joining the constituency political party, having a drink at the pub, spending time in the schools. This slow, grinding, continuous aspect of neighbourhood work had two positive outcomes. First, local confidence in the team was bolstered when it became clear that they were not birds of passage, that they really were committed to the area. Second, over time the staff did perceive what people wanted. For instance, it took over a year before it dawned on me that the greenhouse was an integral part of the youth work because the teenagers just wanted a place of their own. It took even longer for Dave and I to pick up the resentment of the girls that the clubs were gender blind and that there was a demand for activities for young mothers. Once perceived, the appointment of Jane Sellars followed.

Perhaps the most important gain from the long-term nature of the project was that it facilitated lengthy relationships with certain youngsters, and the value of these friendships has already been discussed. An allied aspect is that staying long-term meant that the team grew up with some of the youngsters. Those who, at the beginning, were about ten years old when they joined in the clubs , progressed to be older teenagers while the initial staff were still there. Living so close and so long together, the leaders accumulated a kind of knowledge and emotional bank in regard to the children and young people. Certainly, the staff were more comfortable in coping with stroppy 15–16 year olds when they had dealt with them since they were kids. More, they began to perceive their behaviour patterns: the boy whose withdrawal and moroseness indicated that delinquency was on the way, the deep sadness of another which reflected hurt and arguments at home, the aggressiveness of a girl which meant that her relationship with her boyfriend was on the rocks again. Such warning signs sometimes allowed the staff to take diversionary and preventative measures to avoid the negative actions which usually followed. Occasionally, such knowledge stopped hasty intervention. One volatile girl would storm out of the room screaming that she was running away and would kill herself: over time, the team learned that the threats did not have to be taken seriously and that she always crept back.

It has already been noted that a considerable number of the young people, like some adults, became assistants or helpers. Their involvement owed something to the sheer length of time which they spent with the project. Time gave them the space to identify with the project, to take on some of the leaders' values and approaches, and to grow in personal maturity. Time allowed the leaders to see their potential as helpers. Looking back, it is almost amazing that some of the most disruptive kids later became such valuable assistants. And not just assistants. Thelma and Colin, both of whose difficulties have been aired in these pages, later served the project as full-time members of staff.

Lastly, it was over time that the staff grew alongside families. The leaders developed alongside the children but the children were never regarded as separate from their families. As the years went by, the leaders found that they were often drawn into the ups and downs of family life. To cite Thelma's family again. Thelma was one of the first members of the youth club but the family contact was really made when her mother, Molly, and her baby, came to Jane's group. Molly later asked me to speak with Thelma about her behaviour but the main friendship was between Jane and Thelma. Then Molly became a leading helper at the play schemes. When the marriage got into difficulties, Jane spent much time with all the parties, advising Molly and supporting the children who were devastated by the split up of their parents. Jane also gave the husband much practical support as he continued to look after one of the younger children. In turn, he too became a volunteer at the project. Thus the work with the youngsters merged into what was almost a family service. But not a one-sided service. The project served the family yet the same family produced two capable volunteers and a full-time member of staff. Such outcomes can not come about in a few months. They require years and years and, if nothing else, the Southdown Project was successful in sticking there.

Long-termism is not a characteristic of the staff of many British social services. Ray Jones, speaking as an experienced director of a local authority department and one who has placed large contracts with national voluntary societies, points out that both these kinds of organisations put an emphasis on professional staff. Yet, he added, 'Professionals tend not to have strong community links because they do not usually live where they work and are likely to move from one place to another as they pursue their careers. By contrast, when workers are recruited from their communities, they are often not looking to a career but to having a job and keeping their local links going. Therefore they stay and so ensure continuity'. In other words, the project's long-termism was closely linked with the fact that it was also rooted in the neighbourhood.

Contributory Factors

In addition to the above primary factors, three other items contributed to the effectiveness and durability of the Southdown Project.

Firstly, in terms of strategy, it opted for a mixed not a specialist approach. It did not concentrate just on, for instance, offenders, children of lone parents or drug abusers. To do so would have had three adverse knock on effects.

- Persons cast into one negative role may tend to take on the attitudes and behaviour which confirm it. For example, if certain teenagers are designated as delinquents and then treated just in the company of other delinquents, then they may well behave as delinquents.

- Other residents might well have resented the attention given to one grouping and the neglect of others.

- Neighbours might well have been disturbed if the project had identified with one unpopular kind of clientele and to have considered that it cast a stigma over their area.

Instead, the project was developed as a neighbourhood one open to any youngsters on the basis of living in the area. Of course, this was not meant to deter those who did struggle with severe personal problems. But they came to the project through a broad door which was open to anyone. To enter the house or the building was not to be marked out as a needy person because many called just to borrow a tent, make a phone call or for a game of table tennis etc. Moreover, the fact that the project majored on ordinary youth clubs meant that those who did have acute troubles mixed with those who did not. In teenage, peers are probably the strongest influence on young people so it was important that those who did steal, truant, run away etc. mixed freely with those who did not.

Second, the Southdown Project enjoyed positive relationships with teachers, social workers and police persons. Senior teachers would phone the project leaders if youngsters attached to the project had not turned up or were beyond control. Social workers and police often dropped informally into the project building and out of these contacts came joint football, cricket and darts matches. By mixing with the officials in a leisure atmosphere, the youngsters began to see them in a different, more positive light. The contacts also led to co-operative action in order to divert certain youngsters away from trouble, to keep them out of the courts and out of care. Such co-operation, however, only proceeded with the explicit permission of the individuals concerned. Today, in Easterhouse, Glasgow, I sometimes look back enviously at the degree of joint work. Certainly, the schools here welcome in the staff from our project. But social workers and police officers rarely come into the project. This is not because they are unwilling or uninterested.

Rather it is because they are so overwhelmed by the sheer volume of immediate child abuse and crime crises that they have no time for the informal and often out-of-hours contacts which were a feature of the work in Southdown.

Third, in terms of external opportunities, the Southdown youngsters did have job prospects. Although some found difficulty in finding employment, most did so even if it was after a period on job schemes. They could thus move on to a wage, to the means of buying leisure, and later to independence and adult status. The study of Wynn in the last chapter shows how crucial it was that this former delinquent found a satisfying post where he soon achieved promotion. By contrast, unemployment has long been a built-in feature in Easterhouse and, on leaving school, many youngsters have faced unemployment or grotty job schemes which do not lead to meaningful and permanent jobs. The upshot has been a pool of young people with little money and little to do who are then vulnerable to falling deeper into trouble rather than getting out of it. I am not asserting that Southdown had all the advantages. On the contrary, our project in Easterhouse has found it much easier to obtain grants.

To sum up. The Southdown Project offered three important services to youngsters.

- Clubs, trips and holidays which were enjoyed by many;
- The semi-independence of the greenhouse which became the base for teenagers;
- Individual relationships for those with personal difficulties.

The impact of these services was maximised by four primary factors.

- The residence of the leaders in the area;
- The style of their leadership;
- The support of the community;
- A commitment to staying long-term.

Also important were three contributory or secondary factors.

- A mixed rather than a specialist approach;
- Positive co-operation with other agencies;
- Access to jobs for youngsters.

The combination of the services and factors did not mean that the Southdown Project could help all the youngsters it encountered. But it did mean that it improved the quality of childhood for many ordinary children on the estate and enabled some others to overcome severe problems which might have marred their adult lives.

Chapter Seven

Government and Neighbourhood

The Southdown Project was at its height during the 1970s and 1980s when governments, both Labour and Conservative, were worried about the rise of juvenile delinquency and the decline of the traditional family. Today former Southdown young people find themselves as adults under the government of New Labour whose social concerns echo that of its predecessors. Jack Straw, the Home Secretary, wrote in a government consultation document *Supporting Families,* 'Families are under stress. The divorce rate has risen sharply. There are more children being brought up in single parent families, and there is more child poverty, often as a direct consequence of family breakdown. Rising crime and drug abuse are indirect symptoms of problems in the family'. (1998, p 4) The Home Secretary is convinced that many of the problems of youth; vandalism, offending, truancy, low educational attainment, drug abuse, teenage pregnancies etc. stem from inadequate parenting. He has spearheaded an attack both to counter juvenile crime and to strengthen family life.

Dealing with Juvenile Crime.

As Home Secretary, Jack Straw soon implemented the previous government's plans for secure training centres for 12–14 year olds and repeatedly declared that he would be 'tough on crime.' He guided through the Crime and Disorder Act (1998), most of which applied to England and Wales. Many of its praiseworthy sections, particularly those against racially-aggravated offences, cannot be covered here. Overall, it claimed to strike a balance between preventing and punishing delinquency. Amongst the provisions most relevant to this chapter are the following:

1. The Act stated that it 'shall be the principal aim of the youth justice system to prevent offending by children and young persons' (Section 37). This duty was placed upon local authorities with other bodies being expected to co-operate with them.

2. Local authorities were given a duty to establish youth offending teams to include social workers, probation officers, police officers and education and health staff. Their main purpose was 'to co-ordinate the provision of youth justice services for all those in the authority's area who need them'. (Section 39)

3. It established a Youth Justice Board for England and Wales with responsibility to co-ordinate the creation of a national framework for dealing with young offenders and to monitor performances of youth justice agencies.

4. Parenting Orders were introduced under which parents can be required to attend counselling or guidance in order to improve their supervision of children.

5. Local authorities were empowered to impose local child curfews on children under ten years of age.

6. Detention and Training Orders were set up as a new custodial sentence involving detention and training for young offenders followed by a period of supervision.

7. Young Offender Remand. Courts were empowered to remove children and young people aged 12 and over to local authority secure accommodation. 15–16 year old boys who met certain criteria could be remanded to prison.

Following the Act, Lord Warner was appointed as chairman of the Youth Justice Board. It had an initial three year budget of £85 million to establish innovative local projects and to oversee the Youth Offending Teams, 60 of which were in place by mid-1999. Lord Warner specified the government's approach as follows:

- The swift administration of justice so that every young person accused of breaking the law has the matter resolved without delay.
- Punishment proportionate to the seriousness and persistence of offending.
- Earlier intervention in the lives of young people and their families; interventions that tackle the particular factors, e.g. family, personal, social, education, health, that put the young person at risk of further offending.
- Reinforcing the responsibilities of parents. (Warner, 1999)

New Labour's stated intention to prevent delinquency is welcome indeed and gives an emphasis not marked under the previous government. The establishment of Youth Offending Teams, appointed by the Chief Executives of local authorities, signals that juvenile crime is being taken seriously. Hopefully, the new multi-disciplinary teams will ensure that help is available to vulnerable youngsters no matter where they live. But I am disappointed that the government's strategy takes little note of the lessons of the Southdown Project and other voluntary projects with similar approaches.

First, the government's plans to counter delinquency take little heed of the part which can be played by projects rooted in their own neighbourhoods. The Southdown Project attempted to gain local backing, support and talent by drawing in parents and residents as staff, sessional workers and volunteers. The project grew partly in response to their ideas. The Home Office style is to impose from above. Of course, to a certain extent, the government has to adopt a top-down approach in that it proposes and passes legislation. But this legislation could have done much more to stimulate local initiatives and to profit from local knowledge and experience. The apex of the new system is a Youth Justice Board chaired by a Lord and made up of highly paid professionals. It has little room for people who experience delinquency at first hand because they reside in socially deprived areas, particularly council estates. It has no places for those who have been delinquents. Dave Wiles would have been an ideal member.

Similarly, the Youth Offending Teams are dominated by professionals and officials who decide what their area needs and what kind of projects are to be launched. It must be acknowledged that such experts will have the interests of their areas at heart and will contribute much expertise. However, the teams do not have to include residents of the very localities where delinquency is highest and hence the plans which are set in motion may well be regarded as distanced and possibly as irrelevant. Further, projects conceived in this fashion tend to be run by professionals who commute in and out of the areas. The Southdown Project and others have demonstrated the advantages of having staff who live in the localities, who identify with the neighbourhoods and whose commitment is soon perceived.

A centralised, highly regulated, top-down approach may also engender excessive bureaucracy. Already a report by the Audit Commission called *Mis-spent Youth* has indicated that youth justice workers spend a majority of their time on administration and meetings, (1998). One of the benefits of the Southdown Project was that the Children's Society gave it great freedom on how to function so that the leaders had to attend few outside meetings while administration was kept to a minimum. In addition, the staff were on the spot where youngsters could reach them easily. The outcome was that a large proportion of the staff's time was spent in direct contact with young people.

Second, the Home Office strategy places no emphasis on the value of long-term projects. The Youth Offending Teams are setting up three year initiatives. Some are bolstered by government money which will cease after three years so there is a reluctance to go beyond short-term planning. Yet this study has established that a vital ingredient of the Southdown Project was that the staff stayed at least ten years, that they became a part of the community, that they grew up with local families. It was over this lengthy period that they developed and displayed the characteristics that appealed to youngsters and which became the basis of resourceful friendship.

Third, the government does not give priority to a mixed or neighbourhood-wide approach. Its talk is of 'intensive intervention' on 'high risk' youngsters and their parents. I am not suggesting that special treatment limited to a few offenders and their families will be without benefits. I am pointing out that the Southdown Project devised an alternative approach based on the belief that offenders and potential offenders could be helped by integrating them within activities open to the whole neighbourhood. The leaders argued that such integration was useful because:

- It did not stigmatise youngsters by marking them out as delinquents or deviants.

- It allowed them to mix with and to be influenced by peers who were not 'at risk'.
- It won local support for the project from neighbours who would have disliked activities restricted to a few youngsters and which excluded the majority.

Fourth, the government legislation seems unaware of the dangers of swift intervention. The get tough policy is about getting offenders quickly to court and then, with its USA catch phrase of 'three strikes and you're out', of facilitating custody if offences are repeated. This approach is founded on the expectation that a get tough approach, along with the threat of and the experience of custody, will deter and cure offenders. The penal expert Paul Cavadino foresees 'a sharp and undesirable increase in the locking up of children, particularly those under 15', (1998). His dismay is based on evidence that removing youngsters from their homes and neighbourhoods and placing them in institutions with other offenders actually increases their subsequent rates of offending. Certainly, the push to get children and young people into courts and institutions seems at variance with the government's stated intention of preventing delinquency. The leaders of the Southdown Project were convinced that, as far as possible, it was best to contain youngsters who displayed anti-social behaviour within their own neighbourhoods, where they could be influenced by the more positive values, behaviour and friendships of adults and peers. Simultaneously they would not suffer the trauma of being separated from their own families. It worked. For instance, Wynn, Adam and Arnold committed a string of offences and, under the Home Office's present approaches, would have been continually in court and then put in custody. Wynn was in court just as he left school and if sent away to approved school would have missed out on the job which was to make him a stable and productive citizen. The project leaders worked continually to keep Adam and Arnold in the community and they both acknowledged that otherwise they would have gone into custody and then probably to prison as adults. Of course, at times a few youngsters do have to undergo custody in order to protect others. None the less, the experience of the Southdown Project suggests that a project with its characteristics can succeed in diverting vulnerable youngsters away from trouble and custody. The project would have found it much harder to do so under the present government's favoured emphasis on quick and severe punishment. None the less, the Act does state that prevention is important. So it is unfortunate that the present Home Secretary offers no backing to projects which are long-term, which are run by residents, which function by drawing in a wide range of youngsters and which, therefore, have much to contribute to prevention.

Supporting Families

Jack Straw, along with other New Labour politicians, constantly blames the anti-social behaviour of youngsters on their parents, on their poor examples, lack of morals, insufficient discipline, inability to help them with school work, on the damage wrought on the children by their divorces and separations, and by their lack of commitment to marriage. He has therefore devised a series of programmes to improve parenting and family life. It is worth noting that these programmes seem directed at the kind of parents who live on council estates and inner ring areas. Many senior politicians have affairs, divorce, remarry, have difficulties with their children. Yet somehow no blame is directed at them. They are not exhorted to remain in lifelong relationships with their spouses. They will not be subjected to parenting orders, they will not have to attend parenting groups, their children will not be at risk of custody. Noticeably, when Mr Straw's own son was caught in the possession of drugs, he was not 'swiftly' brought before the courts. Indeed, he was never prosecuted. I make these points not to decry any programmes which strengthen family life. Far from it. It is rather to point out that low-incomed citizens are not fools and they do perceive the social bias in programmes and policies which are intended to improve their parental functioning but which are not applied to those at the top.

None the less, to Jack Straw's credit he is concerned about the stability of family life. As chairman of the Ministerial Group on the Family, he has been the driving force of a government publication *Supporting Families* which brings together a whole host of initiatives aimed at improving parenting and marriage, (1998).

Four seem particularly significant.

- The New Family and Parenting Institute. With a three year grant of £2 million and a chief executive on a salary of up to £60,000, the Institute is to improve parenting by developing 'parenting support programmes' and by disseminating information about how to be good parents.

- In 1999, the government launched Parentline with a budget of £1 million over three years. It provides free advice to parents over the phone.

- Sure Start is aimed particularly at parents with small children. The £540 million budget over three years will encourage local partnerships to set up services to improve the health, the day care, the play and the early learning of young children and their parents.

- Family Support Grants. In 1999, Jack Straw announced £1 million of grants to agencies such as the Thomas Coram Foundation, the Family Policy Studies Centre and NCH Action for Children. A further £3 million was to be open to bids in the next two years.

In addition, *Supporting Families* acknowledged that poverty can undermine family life and pointed to changes being wrought by other government departments with particular mention of improvements in levels of Child Benefit and the introduction of the Working Families Tax Credit.

Elsewhere I have argued that the explanation of children's anti-social behaviour is associated with, but is not confined to, inadequate parenting, (1995, part 1). Further, I am not convinced that the government's measures do constitute an effective attack on poverty and inequality, (1999). However, like most people I desire to see our society characterised by caring parents and stable relationships which do provide the social and emotional framework in which children can thrive in ways which are satisfactory to society, to their parents and to themselves. The question is whether the government approach, as set out in *Supporting Families*, is sufficient.

Any initiatives to support families are to be welcomed and it is not disputed that the government's programmes will help some parents. Certainly they are equipped with enormous resources, will have numerous qualified staff and the keen backing of government ministers. But, again, the tenor of these initiatives is that the well-paid experts on high possess all the knowledge and skills and that those at the bottom who lack them should accept their guidance. Unfortunately, the attitudes conveyed within this process can often increase the recipients' sense of inferiority and make it difficult for them to receive help. The government and its advisors do not seem to appreciate that low-incomed residents of council estates and other deprived areas frequently have a problem with outsiders who travel in with their advice about parenting but have no ongoing experience of what it is like to raise children in circumstances of social deprivation. They do not understand that when partnerships of statutory and large voluntary societies decide to make bids for the latest government pots of gold, which they then decree will be used for services in the neighbourhoods they designate, by staff they appoint and with methods they decide, they may well be widening the divide between them and vulnerable families. I speak having once got my fingers burnt. When I moved to Easterhouse in Glasgow, I came with some financial backing from a national voluntary society. In the early months, I did little except to hang about the area and mix with residents who were getting together in an abandoned shop. They welcomed my involvement but soon made it clear that they did not want money or direction from outside agencies. They had seen it before. They had experienced outside children's organisations coming in, starting something on their terms, and then leaving after three years. They were right and I now acknowledge that the success of the local body which was set up owes much to its independence.

To repeat, I hope and expect that the government initiatives will be of use to some families. Much will depend on whether they can convince residents that they are unreservedly on their side and that they come not to extend the empires of outside charities but to serve and to stay with families. What is most regrettable is that the government gives no encouragement to alternative approaches. The Southdown Project grew from inside. Its mother and toddlers' groups started when the mothers requested them. They saw that a house was available, that Jane would be willing to organise it and that it could be of benefit to them as parents. This is very different from officials being sent in with a brief to set up groups for inadequate parents. Further, the Southdown Project was characterised by parents offering their services as volunteers and then gaining confidence in themselves as they succeeded at certain tasks. The emphasis was the positive one of using their strengths, not zooming in on their failures. It worked. Yet the government has chosen to ignore the potential of, and lessons from, such small projects. It has distributed Family Support Grants to large voluntary bodies, including those already with incomes of millions of pounds and further millions in their reserves, but not to small neighbourhood projects and not to low-incomed residents who could have started their schemes, tailored to their areas.

I advocate that the government should extend its ways of supporting families. As well as the millions it is spending on high profile initiatives and high salaried professionals, it should ensure funding for small, local projects with the following characteristics.

- They are rooted in neighbourhoods, have the support and involvement of residents, and are responsive to the kind of activities which they see as important.
- They are long-term with staff living in the area.
- They are positive in the sense that they first, give priority to keeping youngsters with their parents, to helping with their education and jobs and second, that they treat parents not as recipients, but as helpers who have something to give.

At present small, local projects are financially neglected. Central government will make huge grants to national voluntary societies but declares that small projects are the responsibility of the local authorities. Unfortunately local authorities are not always willing or able to make grants to them. Once the Southdown Project gained independence from the Children's Society, it endured enormous financial problems and limited help from the local authority so that it was eventually brought to its knees. Today, local authorities are even less generous towards local projects. Their budget for voluntary grants is often deployed to finance contracts with national voluntary societies to carry out duties previously undertaken directly by their own employees. Simultaneously, and because of reductions in the amounts received from central government, several urban local authorities have had to make cuts and small projects are an easy target. In Glasgow, a senior councillor Des McNulty stated that the cuts:

> *target more clearly on some of the weakest and most vulnerable communities and grants in the city. The total budget for voluntary sector projects aimed at needy groups, which in the past would have amounted to £8–9 million over the next three years, has been slashed to just £2.1 million – a cut of 76 per cent.* (cited by Holman, 1998)

Not surprisingly, some groups and projects in the areas of highest need have closed down. Fortunately, a number of charitable trusts are prepared to support locally rooted projects. But they are overwhelmed with applications and can only meet the financial requests of just a few.

My proposal is that the government should finance a National Neighbourhood Fund which would distribute money to Neighbourhood Trusts in the most deprived areas. In turn, the Trusts would make grants to small, local projects and groups. Residents of the areas would elect members of their Trusts. The Trusts would elect representatives to the National Neighbourhood Fund. The system would give more financial security to existing projects and allow more to get started: it would stimulate locally run services capable of strengthening young people and families: it would reduce unemployment by providing jobs for residents who are frequently the very people best equipped to organise local services.

I believe that a National Neighbourhood Fund should be financed from taxation just as MPs receive generous salaries and expenses and members of the House of Lords obtain daily allowances from public funds. However, I acknowledge that the present government has decreed that it will not increase income tax even on those citizens with incomes of over £70,000 a year. So I make another proposal. Poor people pay proportionately more into the National Lottery than affluent people despite the fact that much of the proceeds go on causes from which they obtain no benefit, for instance, the Greenwich Millennium Dome, the Tate Gallery, posh rowing clubs and sports centres located within public schools. My suggestion is that all the money paid into the National Lottery from deprived areas be directed back into them for allocation by Neighbourhood Trusts.

Nearly a quarter of a century since the Southdown Project was started, its impact is still remembered and still felt by many of the young people who attended it. The 51 former members, now adults, are agreed that it provided them with leisure activities which they would otherwise have missed, with friendships, with individual relationships with adults they trusted. Some are convinced it steered them away from crime and other anti-social behaviour. Some believe that its influence, values and practices stayed with them into adulthood. The claim of this study is not that the approach adopted by the Southdown Project is the only or the best means of supporting young people in socially deprived areas. It does claim that it is one very useful way which was appreciated by those who used it. Unfortunately, the project's basic ingredients, the combination of clubs with resourceful friendships, staff living in the area, priority to local involvement, staying long-term and an emphasis on prevention rather than intervention, are not fashionable today and so receive little backing from central and local government. But if a National Neighbourhood Fund or a reformed National Lottery were to support such projects, then a new generation of youngsters would benefit in like manner to their predecessors on the Southdown estate. As one group at the Southdown reunion recorded, 'We would want it for our kids'.

Postscript

While checking the manuscript of this book, I received a six page letter from a young man in remand prison. I had been trying to track him down to interview him for this study. It is too late to include him in the numerical analysis but his experience is still relevant. Moreover, book or no book, I am just glad to be in touch with him again.

He featured in *Kids at the Door* as Daniel. He was brought up by a lone mother who loved him but could not control him. As a youngster, he came regularly to the clubs and to our house where he displayed a mixture of charm and aggression. On one occasion, Dave and I had taken some boys to a youth games tournament. Daniel and another boy were just out for trouble, shoplifting and picking fights. Eventually we had to take them home. I drove as Dave forcibly prevented Daniel from jumping out of the minibus. Once in his house, he refused to listen to anyone, jumped through the window and attempted to attack me with a garden fork. A few days later, he knocked on our door to make his peace. When he was charged with robbery, Dave and I accompanied him to court for there was a bond between us. He had a likeable, talented side which was marred by the verbal and physical abuse which erupted within him. As he grew older, he spent a good deal of time in the house. He was at his best when in a small group, he seemed threatened by newcomers or larger numbers.

After I left Southdown, I lost contact with Daniel, although I heard that he had been sent to a detention centre. But I never forgot him, always asked after him and, when I revisited Southdown, I made considerable efforts to find him. Eventually, his sister provided the link. She sent Daniel my address and I received his letter. He had not been to prison before but, facing charges of violence, said he was expecting to be sentenced for up to four years.

His letter detailed the course of his life since we last met. In his early twenties, he had a job, married and two children. The marriage was extremely volatile but, he wrote, 'I stayed with her because I didn't want to split up with my children like my dad did to me'. However, he did succumb to heroin and, before long, had lost his job and wife. The following years saw a kind of nightmare in which he was homeless, dealt in drugs, fell foul of violent criminals, nearly died when stabbed by a syringe full of heroin, was beaten up with a hammer and deliberately run down by a car. Three of his closest friends died from drug-related causes and brought him to his present point of 'an emotional and physical wreck.' Yet through it all, he tried to maintain contact with his children, with his sister and mother.

In this book, I may have given too rosy a picture about the effectiveness of the Southdown Project. Daniel's story should make me more cautious. It is a reminder that such projects are not a wonder solution, that some youngsters had a close association with it and yet did not steer clear of emotional instability, crime and drugs. Yet I do not think the links with Daniel were to no avail. He wrote, 'Bob if you hadn't spent the time on me years ago, I'd have been in these places (prison) all my life. I've never really thanked you for what you did for me.'

These are kind words but the fact remains that Daniel's life has been characterised by unhappy personal relationships, by drug abuse and violence. In the face of these distressing experiences, three points can yet be made.

First, Daniel is as valuable as anyone else. As a humanitarian, I believe he is as important as the children of Prince Charles or Tony Blair. As a Christian, I believe that God has a special concern for those who have lacked privileges and luxuries. It follows that the Southdown Project was right to give its services to Daniel. Right not just because he might have been chalked up as a success and as a justification for the methods it pioneered. But right simply because he was a valuable young person who needed adults who could offer him the guidance and the affection which is found in resourceful friendship.

Second, Daniel still has the potential to change. He wrote in his letter, 'You gave me a copy of *Kids at the Door*. I don't know if you can remember what you wrote inside it. I can. It has haunted me for years. *To Daniel. Best wishes from Bob, Dave and Jane. We now think he can make a success of himself.* He added that he still wants to sort out his life and his kids. If that spark of motivation can be fanned by his determination and by the love of others, then he can change. In fact, he did not get sent to prison but was placed on two years probation. I am planning to visit him and, at least, he can know that his former youth club leaders still believe he can make a success of himself.

Third, the Southdown Project does not end. Within its life span, it facilitated the establishment of friendships between adults and young people and between youngsters and other youngsters. Dave, Jane and I are wanting to maintain our friendship with Daniel. But the facilitation was not easy. It depended upon people committing themselves long-term, upon staff living in the area, upon residents giving their support. If these features can be replicated then more Southdown Projects can be created and more young people can benefit, as did the majority of those who came to the project. Not least, it will also lead to ties so strong that the relationships outlive the institution. They are the kind of relationships which will always embrace people like Daniel.

References

Audit Commission (1998). *Mis-spent Youth*.

Bebbington, A., and Miles, J. (1989). The Background of Children who Enter Local Authority Care. *British Journal of Social Work*, Vol. 19; No. 5: 349–368.

Bell, C. and Newby, H. (1971). *Community Studies*. Allen and Unwin.

Bishop, N. (1998). *Can Christian Based Youth Clubs Reduce Deviancy?* University of Portsmouth.

Cavadino, P. (1998). The Law Disordered. *Community Care*, 28 May–3 June.

Cockett, M. and Tripp, J. (1994). *The Exeter Family Study*. University of Exeter Press.

Dennis, N. and Erdos, G. (1992). *Families Without Fatherhood*. Institute of Economic Affairs.

Henderson, P. (Ed.) (1995). *Children and Communities*. Pluto Press.

Holman, B. (1981). *Kids at the Door*. Basil Blackwell.

Holman, B. (1983). *Resourceful Friends*. Children's Society.

Holman, B. (1995). *Children and Crime*. Lion Publishing.

Holman, B. (1998). Neighbourhoods and Exclusion. In Barry, M. and Hallett, C. (Eds.). *Social Exclusion and Social Work*. Russell House Publishing.

Holman, B. (1999). A Voice from the Estate. In Dale, G. (Ed.). *Joined-up Writing*. New Labour and Social Inclusion, Christian Socialist Movement.

Home Office (1998). *Supporting Families*. Stationery Office.

Jones, R. (1983) Living and Working on the Patch. *Community Development Journal*, Vol. 18, No. 1: 10–19.

Kolvin, I. *et al.* (1991). *Continuities of Deprivation*. Avebury.

Rutter, M., Giller, H. and Hagell, A. (1999). *Antisocial Behaviour by Young People*. Cambridge University Press.

Utting, D., Bright, J. and Henricson, C. (1993). *Crime and the Family*. Family Policy Studies Centre.

Utting, D. (1995). *Family and Parenthood*. Joseph Rowntree Foundation.

Wadsworth, M. (1979). *The Roots of Delinquency*. Martin Robertson.

Warner, N. (1999). Tackling Youth Justice. *Professional Social Work*, June.

West, D. (reprinted 1968). *The Young Offender*, Pelican.

West, D. and Farrington, D. (1977). *The Delinquent Way of Life*. Heinemann.

Wiles, D. (1990). Taped interview for Open University Course, Working with Children and Young People.

Willmott, P. (revised edition 1969). *Adolescent Boys of East London*. Pelican.

Wilson, H. (1987). Parental Supervision Re-Examined. *British Journal of Criminology*, Vol. 27; No. 3: 275–301.

Wilson, H. and Herbert, G. (1978). *Parents and Children in the Inner City*. Routledge and Kegan Paul.